Five Ps Leading Teams to Top Results

OL VER'S SPOT

FOR THE PUBLIC SECTOR

A LEADERSHIP STORY

Dr. Patrick Leddin, PMP

Author photo by Susan Speece

ISBN: 1470119005
ISBN-13: 9781470119003

Contents

Introduction

Every year, governments invest millions, if not billions, of dollars to increase employee effectiveness and reduce inefficiencies. Computer systems sporting acronym-laden names and continual reorganization efforts often lead the pack. At times, desired results are achieved and the investment is validated. However, all too often initiatives die on the vine due to leadership changes and lack of continued funding, or the muffled conversation that the effort should have never started in the first place eventually wins the day.

If people can be bold enough to suggest that there can be a world without hunger, war, or poverty, why can't we agree that there can be a government with engaged, committed, and customer-focused employees? This book contends that the answer lies not in new sweeping changes to policies, processes, or procedures. All too often, these efforts gum the works, slow progress, squander resources, and cause workers to dig deeper into their anti-change fighting positions.

Instead of sweeping changes and reforms, a commitment to developing leaders and teams that drive accountability, commitment, and engagement is needed. If the desired efficiencies are to be truly achieved, governments must rethink business as usual and embrace pragmatic and arguably more effective efforts. Successful accomplishment of strategy doesn't happen in the highest government offices or bodies of legislation. It happens at the front line where individual employees and their leaders interact and make decisions about how to employ resources every day. Unless that part is done correctly, no strategy, no matter how grand it is, matters.

This story discusses how one group of leaders in one government agency worked to get it right. The story is a work of fiction, and the characters exist only in the author's mind. However, the five steps outlined in this book are grounded in reality and represent how leaders and their teams can work together to accomplish amazing results. Many government leaders and employees don't operate under this simple five-step process. It isn't because they are bad people who don't want to perform well. It's simply that most of them operate in a system that over time erodes their passion for excellence. Governments will be far more effective when frontline employees and their leaders embrace a simple planning and execution approach.

A Leadership Story

Chapter 1: A New Reality

There's that feeling again, Susan Walker thought as she trudged down the narrow hallway. In all honesty, the word hallway was inaccurate. A hallway suggests some sort of permanency. She was navigating a pathway that meandered through the cubicle farm. Divided by four-foot-high walls adorned in a nondescript gray fabric, the path shifted positions occasionally as workspaces were reconfigured, people repositioned, and offices renamed. Moving cubicle walls appeared to be a never-ending process that slowly weaved its way through the entire organization only to begin again the next year.

Trudging and the associated mixture of feelings—doubt, anxiety, and a dash of fear—did not come naturally to Susan. Typically the most upbeat person in a room, she was known for her contagious smile and her ability to share kind words. Infusing energy and positivity into daily interactions was her calling card, but even she had her limits, and they were being tested. As she closed in on the conference room, her mind continued to question the situation. *How is it possible that I feel so anxious and out of place in an organization where I've worked for years?*

With the question barely formed in her mind, she turned the corner, entered the conference room, and observed that the Monday morning staff meeting was about to start. Susan scanned her colleagues' faces, recognizing the all too common mixture of frustration and apprehension. Her gaze settled on Michael Thomas, the tall and impeccably dressed chief of Plans and Policy, and the two briefly made eye contact as he slid into his usual seat. Michael's hesitant nod of solidarity confirmed Susan's belief that she was not alone in her concern. Susan offered an uncomfortable smile in response.

The weekly gathering had been a Monday morning eight a.m. staple for years. Operating on autopilot, she settled into her normal spot at the table. Her trusty coffee mug, filled to the brim with the required dose of morning caffeine, transitioned from her hand to the worn conference table as if it knew the routine. Familiar banter filled the room as her colleagues discussed the arrival of spring and the warm weather and flurry of weekend activities it brought with it. The conversations were comforting, but all recognized that beneath common dialogues lurked the beginning of another uncomfortable session that had become all too regular over the past few months.

It's only been ninety days, Susan thought. *How is it possible that so much has changed?* Just three short months earlier, she had passed the four-year mark as the agency's chief of Human Resources (HR) and fifteen years as a government employee. Gifted in a number of areas, she was most talented as a relationship builder. Her cheery disposition, combined with genuine concern for others and great listening skills, made her a sounding board for her colleagues as they struggled to make professional and at times personal decisions. In her first forty-eight months as HR manager, Susan grew very comfortable in her position, enjoying both her role and the relationships developed with her team, the organization's 350-plus employees, and her fellow leaders.

Contentment wasn't just reserved for Susan. Until recently, the consistent nature of the jobs throughout the Technology Integration and Development Agency, commonly referred to as TIDA or simply the agency, allowed the vast majority of the workforce to arrive at eight a.m., leave at five p.m. and fill the day with a vast amount of paper shuffling, e-mail responding, and meeting attending.

Susan reflected on the agency's previous director, Barbara Cray. Barbara's departure was the unintended catalyst for many of the changes. Shortly after Ms. Cray's departure, Sam Finch, her trusty deputy director, was named the interim replacement. A plain talker from rural Wisconsin, he was the product of growing up on a dairy farm where he learned the practices of hard work, straight talk, and team building. In his previous role as deputy director, Sam helped lead the organization through a fairly stable period and managed to get things done in his consistent, no-frills way. Funding was consistent, competition for the agency's services nonexistent, and Barbara's boss stayed out of the agency's day-to-day business. However, all that had changed in a dramatic, arguably shocking way. Shortly after Barbara's departure, senior leadership above the agency changed too.

To Sam's surprise, Barbara's departure was part of a larger leadership shuffle. Not only did she get reassigned, her boss was transferred as well. Suddenly, the two leadership positions above Sam were vacant. The first vacancy, Barbara's, was filled by Sam in the short-term until the completion of a formal hiring process. Although Sam was a strong candidate for the position, the process had to be conducted to ensure all interested candidates had the opportunity to apply. The second vacancy was filled by Mr. Alex Morgan. With Mr. Morgan's entry came a level of accountability that Sam, Susan, and the agency's entire leadership team had never experienced. From the beginning, Sam struggled in his interactions with Mr. Morgan and his management approach. A stoic figure who said little and appeared to judge all, Mr. Morgan seemed the antithesis of Sam. An impressive résumé complete with the best educational experiences and powerful positions in both government and private sector, Mr. Morgan had mastered the art of lofty rhetoric, confusing metrics, and intimidation.

Enough about the past, Susan thought to herself. *I need to focus on the present and the task at hand.*

In typical fashion, Sam started the meeting with a few pleasantries in an attempt to calm everyone's nerves and put the group at ease. Although appreciated, all in attendance knew that Sam's efforts were simply postponing the inevitable. They were right; in a matter of moments, the conversation turned to the organization's performance on Mr. Morgan's key metrics. Jane Hudson, the agency's recently installed performance improvement manager, retrieved a large stack of paperwork from her bright red briefcase and distributed a packet to everyone in the room. She appeared emotionless as she started her presentation.

Despite her small frame, Jane packed a verbal punch. Susan and her colleagues often referred to Jane as a condensed version of Mr. Morgan, as she was a smaller, more concentrated edition of the man. Per usual, Jane was dressed, or at least accessorized, in red; Jane demanded attention and results.

Many interpreted Jane's dispassionate demeanor as a reflection of her calculated, no-nonsense approach to her work. They believed that she was simply acting as a surrogate for Mr. Morgan and would use the recently installed metrics program to replace every leader in the room. In reality, the leadership team's assessment was half true. Jane did report directly to Mr. Morgan and was "on loan" to the agency to drive improved performance. They were also right in thinking that if the organization continued to miss established goals, then Jane would likely recommend to Mr. Morgan that he replace Sam and everyone else in the room.

What they did not know was how Jane truly felt about the situation. In earlier years, she would brazenly walk into an organization intending to either fix leadership or replace them. She had the brains and willingness to do whatever she believed the situation dictated and the backing of her boss to make it happen. This approach had served her well; she made a name for herself, and the promotions followed.

Sam first met Jane when he was summoned to Mr. Morgan's office, along with a smattering of his peers, to update the new boss on a number of issues. Sitting in the back of the room waiting for his turn, Sam watched in dismay as the other briefers were subjected to a barrage of questions from both their boss and Jane, who sat to Mr. Morgan's right. Eventually, Sam found himself standing on the receiving end of the duo's attacks. After taking his share of verbal abuse, Sam licked his wounds and worked his way back to the agency in a daze. He replayed the episode a number of times in his mind, acknowledging that he couldn't avoid Mr. Morgan, but he'd do his best to steer clear of Jane Hudson in the future.

Despite Sam's desire to avoid Jane, she had somehow steered herself right into the weekly Monday morning staff meeting. What he didn't realize was that Jane was not thrilled about it either.

Had someone observed Jane walking to the meeting, they would have noticed a person exhibiting similar discouragement as those around the table. Head down, she plodded toward the conference room carrying her bulging bright red briefcase and an even heavier burden on her shoulders. However, unlike the others in attendance who brought their dejection into the room and parked it around the conference table, Jane chose to leave her doubts and worries at the door and put on the mask of the focused, aggressive professional. She was very much the person her reputation indicated. Mr. Morgan sent her to get a job done and she was going to do it, no matter the collateral damage. However, unlike past organizations Mr. Morgan had dispatched her to fix, she truly liked this group and wanted to see them be successful. She saw potential in Sam, admiring his passion and the manner in which he interacted with his team. It was this admiration that drove her to be even more focused and direct. After all, that was how she had gotten things done in the past, and she was going to bring her best to help this leadership team. If nothing else, she was going to instill the importance of improving their performance. She may have hoped for them to succeed and was willing to give them the information they needed to run their organization more effectively, but ultimately success lay in the hands of the seven people in the room and the 350 or so staff who reported to them.

Always the perfectionist without an item out of place, Jane adjusted her jacket to ensure that just the right amount of shirt cuff was exposed. She began. "Last quarter this agency missed twenty-one of the twenty-four established metrics." She paused to allow her comments to settle on all in attendance and surveyed the dejected faces in the room. As she continued, Mel Taylor, the once jovial, now painfully unhealthy and increasingly agitated operations manager, let out a sigh that seemed to express the group's collective sentiment.

The leaders watched as Jane presented one confusing performance chart after another. "Frankly, the next quarter is not looking any better. The lead indicators we have in place suggest that the low performance will continue. The agency's Six Sigma projects are way behind schedule, and most metrics, including number seven, 'Incremental Return on Invested Capital,' and number fourteen, the 'Employee Productivity Index,' are moving in the wrong direction. Plus, it's my understanding that several key supervisors and employees will be out in the coming months for required training. Combine these absences with projected personnel losses and the situation will only get worse. I assure you that Mr. Morgan is very concerned with the agency's performance and is not one to accept mediocrity."

Ouch! Susan thought. *Mediocrity? That stings.*

Jane continued to talk, and Susan's mind began to wander. Her mental escape was not from lack of concern. She cared greatly about the future of the organization and its employees. She had simply heard the "bad news" so often that the escape served as a coping mechanism to deal with the stress brought on by these meetings. Jane's monologue continued for the better part of thirty minutes. As the meeting drew to a close, Jane reminded them of the need to "meet the numbers" and "improve performance." She ended with a finishing blow: "Mr. Morgan has told me several times that this agency truly needs to embrace excellence."

When Jane finished her presentation, Sam regained control of the meeting and worked to end on a positive note. "Look folks," Sam began, "I know we're going through some tough times. Jane has painted an ugly picture for us. We can't hide from it. We need to show some improvements quickly. Each of you knows what needs to be done, so just get out there and do it…" Sam's words trailed off, and the leaders began to slowly rise and work their way out of the room.

Walking to the door, Bill Engleman, the agency's chief of Budget and Finance, kept playing Sam's last words over in his mind. *Each of you knows what needs to be done, so just get out there and do it*. He wondered if he really knew what needed to be done. So much had changed. He felt as if the new performance metrics were paralyzing him, his team, and the entire organization. Past leaders had used metrics like system up-time and time-to-resolution to measure agency performance. These were easy to understand and people knew how to connect their daily work to them, but Mr. Morgan's metrics seemed overly complicated and disconnected from everyone's daily work.

Bill walked out the door and right into the "meeting after the meeting." He joined the conversation, and the group huddled in the hallway grew as the leaders came out of the room. Terse statements suggested that most were frustrated with the situation. Sensing their

Chapter 2: Reflection

Sam Finch made a quick departure from the staff meeting. He paid little attention to his leadership team gathered in the hallway as he rapidly covered the distance between the conference room and his office. After a brief stop at his assistant's desk to check messages, his schedule confirmed that he was due to meet with Mr. Morgan in an hour for the weekly senior leadership session, or as Sam called it, "the grilling."

Sam hustled into his office, collapsed in his chair, and reached for his keyboard. A quick touch brought his computer back to life. He entered his obligatory password and watched his e-mail inbox fill with twenty-seven new messages since he had left his desk ninety minutes earlier. Eight of them were marked high priority. "And they told us technology was going to make our lives easier," Sam muttered to himself.

He pushed back from his computer, rose to his feet, and walked across the room. The photo on the wall caught his eye, and he paused for a moment to enjoy the image from his family's farm and reflect on his not-so-distant retirement when he would return to his homestead. He moved to his office doorway and looked out at the office space. From his vantage point, he could see most of the cubicle maze that made up their fifth-floor presence. Several people walked through the space, and an occasional head popped above a cubicle wall and into Sam's line of sight. Their collective voices made an indiscernible noise that inhabited the workspace the entire day. Sam was used to these sounds. He had heard them day in and day out over the last twenty-five or so years as a civil servant.

Sam had been assigned to the agency fifteen years earlier, and other than a two-year stint in another assignment, Sam had spent most of his days—and far too many late nights—working his way from the agency's front line to its front office.

As he watched his colleagues go about their daily work, Sam couldn't help but think that they deserved a better leader. Times were changing. Mr. Morgan was demanding more of the organization, and Sam was unable to insulate his team from the new level of scrutiny they faced. Many times he had thought about retiring, and he had been poised to do so at the end of the year when an unexpected reassignment of the former director changed everything. Suddenly he was in consideration for the position. He was excited about the chance to lead the organization he cared so much about and let it be known that he was very interested. Several other candidates had been identified, but Sam clearly had the upper hand. He felt confident that he would be selected. After all, no one knew the organization as well as he did. His confidence was his demise.

With little preparation, Sam had strolled into the interview session and right into Mr. Morgan's line of fire. The two had yet to meet, and when Mr. Morgan had unleashed a series of questions about the organization's performance over the last several years and the need for transformation, this had revealed Sam's lack of preparation. It was clear that Sam had a good handle on the people in the organization, but his comments on specific performance aspects and anecdotal examples failed to provide the strategic vision, statistical rigor, and overall sophistication Mr. Morgan had expected. Sam left the interview session demoralized. It had felt less like an interview and more like an inquisition, and he knew his performance had been poor. He was not surprised when Mr. Morgan informed him that he was not prepared to appoint Sam as the agency's director, but would name him as the interim director until a "suitable replacement could be found."

Those were Mr. Morgan's exact words.

Sam was constantly reminded of them. They often woke him in the middle of the night, and they consumed his thoughts throughout the day. Deep down, Sam knew that he was the right person for the role. In the beginning, he felt that he could convince Mr. Morgan to place him permanently in the position if given enough time. However, Mr. Morgan's appointment of Jane Hudson as the agency's new performance improvement manager and the organization's performance to date on Mr. Morgan's twenty-four key metrics was wearing on Sam. He estimated that his time in the position was limited to another ninety days if the organization didn't show marked improvement.

Three doors down, Susan Walker was also reflecting on the situation. Her mind returned to the questions she had been asking herself prior to the start of the weekly staff meeting and the conversation she'd had with her colleagues after the meeting. She was considering her career and the situation she found herself and the organization facing.

A flurry of questions swirled in her head. *Did I move up the ranks too quickly? Am I in over my head? Should I work on my résumé and find a new position before things get worse and my choices become limited? How can I leave the organization and the people I care about without a fight?*

Before she could form an answer to any of these questions, there was a knock at her door. She looked up to see Sam. He was on his way to Mr. Morgan's meeting and had stuck his head in to ask about some personnel issues that might come up during "the grilling." Susan gave him the information he requested and took a moment to ask how he was doing. Over the years, the two had formed a trusting relationship, and both felt comfortable confiding in the other. She could tell by the look on his face that he was stressed, and his comments confirmed her assessment. Susan shared that she and her colleagues were equally frustrated, and that they had agreed to meet the next day for lunch to talk over the situation.

At first, Sam was defensive. He questioned what they were up to and why they would meet without him and away from the office. To ease his concerns, Susan invited him to come along. He responded, "Susan, I'm sorry if I questioned everyone's intentions. This whole change in senior leadership and our poor performance is eating at me. Frankly, I'm at a loss. I don't know what to do next. I used to be so confident in my role and the direction of the agency." He paused to collect his thoughts.

Susan jumped in. "Sam, we're all in the same place. That's exactly why we decided to get together, and it's exactly why we chose to do it away from the office. If you're going to be upset at anyone, be upset with me. I'm the one who suggested we meet offsite for lunch." She paused and looked at him earnestly. "To be honest, the 'meeting after the meeting' in the hallway was becoming heated. I didn't want anyone to let their emotions get the best of them, especially in the open where anyone could hear the conversation. We all want to see you succeed." Sam's expression softened. "In fact, it would be wonderful if you could join us tomorrow. I think getting away from the office would be good for all of us."

"I might just take you up on the offer," Sam responded. Looking at his watch, he added, "I've got to go. I don't want to be late for the grilling…I mean meeting." With a quick smile, Sam turned and walked away.

Chapter 3: Short-Notice Gathering

The restaurant was overrun with patrons, but most of the patrons were eating outside. Spring had arrived, and after a long winter, people seemed pleased to enjoy the first warm afternoon of the year. In typical fashion, Susan arrived at the sandwich shop fifteen minutes early. She had a natural desire to take care of people and ensure everyone felt comfortable, so she secured a corner table and began arranging chairs. She had been to the sandwich shop two weeks earlier with her husband and felt that it was the perfect location for the short-notice gathering. The food was good, but more importantly, the restaurant was located a few miles from the office and the table arrangement allowed for private conversation. Susan had hoped to avoid running into other agency employees or have other diners overhear their conversation. Although they weren't going to discuss anything sensitive, Susan felt more comfortable knowing that they were far less exposed than the hallway where the conversation had started.

Susan was relieved to learn that Jane Hudson would not be available for the discussion. Not that Susan would have invited Jane, but the fact that the performance improvement manager was out harassing a different leadership team made things easier. After all, what would Susan have said to her? "Why yes, Jane. We're all going to lunch, but we'd prefer you not tag along. To be honest, most of the discussion will be about you, Mr. Morgan, and the twenty-four metrics the two of you have been beating us up about. In fact, I hope we can get our heads around how to get the agency moving in the right direction and getting you assigned someplace else." Susan was glad she was able to avoid that conversation.

Not surprisingly, Michael Thomas was the first to arrive. Towering above most of the patrons crowding the entrance, Michael was easy to spot. The "Plans and Policy Guy," as Susan called him, was every bit of six foot six. Rumor had it that he was a decent basketball player in college and had made a bit of a name for himself among the avid fans at his alma mater. Susan had no doubt that he was a former athlete as she watched him effortlessly weave his way through the lunch crowd and join her at the table.

As always, Michael was impeccably dressed—dark suit, white dress shirt, and a tie that announced he was abreast of the latest men's fashions. Susan waved him over and invited him to take a seat at the table. Michael secured the chair that would allow him the best view of the restaurant and took a seat.

Since he was a man of few words, Susan was surprised when Michael started the conversation. "Thank you for organizing this meeting. I'm concerned about the direction of the agency, and I'm glad we'll have the chance to talk about the issues as a leadership team without the prying eyes and ears of Ms. Hudson."

"My pleasure. I thought it better that we all got together sooner as opposed to waiting any longer," she responded.

Before either could continue their conversation, Bill Engleman alked up to the table. He explained that Mel Taylor was at the counter placing their orders and that he would hold the table if Susan and Michael wanted to order too.

Ten minutes later the leadership team, including their interim boss, was seated around the table exchanging small talk and eating their meals. Sam waited until all were settled and started the discussion.

"First off, my thanks to Susan for setting up this get-together."

Everyone nodded in agreement.

He continued, "Listen folks, I know that things have been trying the last few months. Mr. Morgan and Ms. Hudson have been pretty hard on the agency. I wish I had the answers for how to best address the situation, but I'm at a bit of a loss. I've known each of you for years, and I trust your judgment. I'd like to hear your thoughts on the situation."

No one at the table was shocked by Sam's approach. Although guarded the last few months, he had always been the type of leader who welcomed—actually encouraged—input from the team. All were glad to see this side of him reappear.

Without hesitation, Mel responded, "I'll go first. To say I'm frustrated with the situation would be an understatement. I've been running operations for several years. I know how things work, and I'm getting pretty tired of having someone from outside our organization constantly telling us we're underperforming." Mel's face got redder and his voice louder as he continued, "I don't know what's going on above us, but if I hear the word 'transformation' one more time, my head's going to explode."

Thinking it might happen at that very moment, Bill Engleman jumped in. "I think I know what Mel is saying. I've been working in the financial management world for years. I'm concerned about some of the metrics they're using to measure our performance and the way they approach interacting with us."

Susan agreed. "You guys are right, and I'll take it a step further. Not only am I frustrated by the situation, but our people are too. They seem to be feeding off of our aggravation, and I'm seeing them focus less and less on their work."

The discussion continued with each leader sharing concerns. They spent the better part of the next half hour venting. After each shared their ideas and concerns, Sam took charge. "I appreciate each of you opening up and sharing your feelings. I'd sum it up by saying that we're all in the same place. As painful as it is to admit, I own much of the blame for our problems. I wish I could go back and change some things, but I can't. I think our best move at this point is to focus on improving Mr. Morgan's twenty-four metrics. I'm open to any thoughts about how to make some positive strides. Remember, my door is always open." Sam paused momentarily as he looked at his watch. "My goodness, time has gotten away from me. I've got to get back to the office for a conference call. Let's plan to do this again soon. Thanks for your time. I value each and every one of you and believe we will work through this together."

Everyone at the table returned the sentiment, conveyed their willingness to keep the dialogue moving, and committed to looking for solutions to the challenges they faced. One by one, they excused themselves from the table. Susan was the last one to leave. As she headed to the door, she paused to reflect on the conversation over the past hour. *Well,* she thought, *we didn't manage to come up with a solution like I'd hoped, but I think it was a good use of time to get the issues on the table and to express our support to Sam.*

She stepped out onto the sidewalk and paused for a moment to enjoy the sun. She started toward her car. Along the way, she passed a bookstore. The sign read "Oliver's Spot." A sticker in the window indicated that the establishment had been a member of the Reader's Guild since 1968. She glanced at her watch and decided she had a moment to look around.

As Susan swung the old door open, an old-fashioned bell announced her arrival. The door's inability to shut squarely suggested the building's advanced age. The creaky floor echoed the sentiment. One glance confirmed that the store was much different from the large bookstore chains. It didn't have a coffee bar, there were no comfy chairs to sit in, and stacks of books signified that organization was not high on the priority list. Deciding that sifting through the piles was more than she had time or energy to tackle, she reached for the doorknob. She paused when she heard a man's voice asking, "May I help you?"

Chapter 4: Chance Meeting

Susan turned to see an older gentleman peering out from behind the cluttered counter. "How can I be of assistance?" he asked again.

"Well, I'm not certain what I'm looking for, and I probably don't have much time. Perhaps I can come back another day," she responded.

"That would be fine," he said, "but I know my way around here pretty well. Why don't you tell me what you are looking for, and I'll see if I can dig it up for you." As he came out from behind the counter, Susan got her first look at Oliver Stanton. He wore a crisp pair of khaki pants and a dark blue shirt. It appeared to be a button-down, but Susan wasn't quite sure as a smock covered most of it. He had a full head of disheveled white hair, and he was squinting at her over a pair of reading glasses. His unkempt hair and strained eyes revealed that he had been deep in thought. All his life people had told him that if you put a book in front of him, a bomb could go off and he wouldn't notice it. The prediction proved true, as he had barely noticed Susan's entrance.

Susan paused to gather her thoughts. Out of desperation from her work predicament or curiosity about this interesting character, she decided to take him up on the offer. "Yes, perhaps you can help me." He took a few steps closer as she continued, "I'm looking for some information. Do you have a section on organizational performance?"

"Absolutely. We have a number of books that address organizational performance. Some are in our management section, and others are kept with our leadership materials. If I may ask, I've noticed that people use the phrase to mean different things. When you say 'organizational performance,' what do you mean?"

Sensing the gentleman's genuine desire to be of assistance, Susan began to clarify her thoughts. "Well, I'm looking for something that will tell me how an organization can work together to accomplish a number of performance metrics." Although she started slowly, the words soon came quickly. "Where I work we're trying to do a number of things as part of our everyday duties. Then we have a laundry list of metrics in place that we are being held accountable to—"

Before she could go any further, Oliver interrupted, "Please excuse my jumping in, but I believe that I'm starting to get an idea of what you are looking for. May I ask a couple of other questions?"

Although not one to be easily offended by the interruption, Susan appreciated his politeness. "Of course," she responded.

Removing his glasses with his left hand and steadying a stack of books with his right, Oliver asked, "When you say a number of metrics, how many are you referring to?"

Without hesitation she blurted out, "Twenty-four!"

"Well, you certainly knew that number." A full smile and brief nod of the head encouraged Susan to continue.

"Of course I do, we hear about them every week," she added.

Oliver raised his left hand, glasses held firmly in his grasp, and motioned for Susan to pause. "And of these twenty-four, are they all equally important, or are some more important than others?"

"That's a great question. I really hadn't thought about it that way." Susan cast her eyes downward as she reflected on his question.

He followed with another. "And when you said that you have the everyday work and then the metrics, does that mean they're in conflict with one another?"

Susan answered, "They sure seem to be. The week usually starts with a meeting that focuses on the twenty-four metrics and whether we *are* or are *not* performing." She paused to consider if she was telling too much to a perfect stranger. Deciding that it was safe to continue, she added, "But soon after the weekly meeting is over, we go back to our normal work. Although we have the desire to improve on the metrics, we never seem to get there."

"Very interesting," Oliver said, almost to himself. "So if I understand you correctly, you have a number of performance measures your organization is supposed to perform against. You also have daily work that seems unrelated to those measures. Even though you want to do well on the measures, you can never seem to get to them because of all the other work that needs to be done. Is that about right?"

"Yes, that sounds about right," Susan answered, half embarrassed.

Recognizing both her sense of embarrassment and the reality that her situation was not unique to her job, he calmly continued, "Who created the performance measures?"

"I'm not exactly certain who specifically created them, but I know they were handed down from people above our organization."

"Hmm...that's interesting," he said, not in a judgmental way but in a manner that suggested he was absorbing what she had told him. "So what happens if your organization manages to win on all the metrics?"

"We get to keep our jobs," she said with a smile.

"Okay, I get that." Oliver smiled in return. "But what's the big win? In other words, if you win on all of the smaller metrics, what's the big thing that happens or doesn't happen?"

"Honestly, I don't really know," she replied.

"You know what," he said with a wink, "until you figure that out and can explain it to your people, everything else doesn't really matter that much." He paused to let his words soak in, and then he continued, "We get a lot of books in here on performance management. I know I've ordered them, stocked them, sold them, and read the majority of them. And you know what? They all say pretty much the same thing." Susan listened intently "I'm more than happy to sell you a book or two. I'm just not sure what they will do for you. Books are helpful, no doubt, but I think you would benefit most from a conversation. If you're interested, I'd be happy to chat with you a bit more."

"Wait a second, aren't you in the bookselling business?" she quipped.

"I'll be honest. Selling books has made a great career from me and I've enjoyed it immensely, but now I'm more interested in helping to solve problems. Some folks even think I'm pretty good at it. Give it some thought, and if you're interested pay me another visit sometime. It would be great to share with you the five steps teams follow to get things moving in the right direction."

"Five steps?" Susan asked.

"Yes, five steps. I've learned from decades of reading books," he said, motioning to the stacks of books surrounding him, "that there are five things organizations do well to drive exceptional performance."

"I have to admit, you have certainly piqued my curiosity."

"I'll tell you what," he said as he searched for a piece of paper on the cluttered countertop. "I'll give you the number here at the store. If you want to come by and discuss this further, give me a call and we can set up a time to chat. You can even bring some other folks along if you want." He tore off the bottom half of a sheet of paper and scribbled down his name and number.

Susan was taken aback by the offer. "Thanks," she said as she glanced at the paper. "So you're Oliver, as in Oliver's Spot?"

"Guilty as charged," he replied.

"Nice to meet you, Oliver. I'm Susan." The words were barely out of her mouth when the bookstore's phone rang. Oliver excused himself to get it. Susan turned and headed for the door.

Step 1: Gain Perspective

Chapter 5: First Impressions

Had someone told her a week earlier that she would have been sitting in the old bookstore the following Thursday afternoon, Susan would have thought that person crazy. However, there she sat, and the only person she considered crazy was herself. Sitting adjacent to her was Bill Engleman, the agency's Budget and Finance manager, who was contemplating his own sanity after already deciding that Susan had lost it. When she talked him into meeting Oliver Stanton, he was skeptical. After arriving at the store, surveying the cluttered shelves, and catching a glimpse of Oliver, he was certain that the pressures of Mr. Morgan's metrics had pushed her over the edge.

When Susan left Oliver's Spot two days earlier, the discussion had intrigued her. On her way back to the office, she had decided that Bill was the one colleague she could confide in about the conversation at the small bookstore. Over the years, Susan and Bill had often bounced ideas off one another. Each found the other to be the type of sounding board every good leader needs. Her attempt to track Bill down proved fruitless. He was buried in a mid-year budget review with no chance of surfacing anytime soon. Even if he had come up for air, she knew better than to try to talk to him on the heels of an afternoon budget session.

The next morning, Susan was standing in front of Bill's desk. She asked for a few minutes of his time, and without giving him an opportunity to object, she launched into the story about the bookstore, its owner, and their brief but interesting conversation. Bill learned that

Susan had tried to talk with him the previous day because she was slightly interested in paying the bookstore another visit. If they had met then, he probably would have talked Susan out of it. There was no changing her mind now. Her desire to visit the bookstore again had grown over the course of the night. By morning, she was resolved to have at least one more conversation with Oliver.

Susan wasn't a bit surprised at Bill's response. What she lacked in skepticism, Bill certainly made up for it. He leaned back in his seat and chuckled as she described her initial interaction with Oliver. "Come on, Susan," he said, his eyes narrowing, "this guy's goal is probably to sell you a dozen books—or better yet, get you to buy two or three for every employee in the agency."

Defending the bookstore owner, Susan retorted that he had had the opportunity to sell her a book the day before and had elected not to. She added that he seemed like a kind older gentleman who really was interested in helping solve their problem. Bill countered that perhaps he was just a lonely old man desperate to drag some people into the store for an afternoon conversation over a cup of coffee. Although she disagreed with Bill's assessment, she wasn't in a fighting mood. She conceded that it was possible that additional time spent at Oliver's Spot might be a waste, but she was willing to run the risk if it meant the possibility of learning something that would make next Monday's staff meeting even a *bit* more bearable.

Her final comment stopped Bill in his tracks. "You can laugh at me if you want and chose not to come, but a few hours invested with Oliver might be a small price to pay if it brings a hint of relief."

Even Bill couldn't disagree with that argument.

When Susan and Bill arrived at the store, Oliver was on the phone and a co-worker was helping a customer at the cash register. Oliver gave them a smile and pointed to the back room, indicating that he would be there in a few minutes. The pair followed his direction and made their way to the "meeting room." As they moved from the public portion of the establishment to the employees-only section, they were not surprised at what they saw. The clutter of the store extended and perhaps intensified in the back room. Both wondered how Oliver got anything done in such a cramped, untidy storage area.

Although the room was messy, it was evident that their host had prepared for the visit by arranging a table and chairs and organizing several stacks of books on an array of topics both on and adjacent to the table. Susan's quick count indicated that there were a dozen stacks with no less than fifteen books. On top of each stack was a five-by-eight index card with a topic hand-printed in all capitals. She walked around the folding table and grabbed a seat next to a large stack of books. Perched at the top was a card that read "Performance Management." Bill sat next to her. He too noted the stacks and read the card on the pile labeled "Scoreboards" to his left.

The two said little to each other. Both were absorbed in their own thoughts and paid no attention to the phone conversation in the other room. They only became aware of the phone call as it reached its conclusion. As he finished the call, Oliver's voice grew louder. "Absolutely, it's my pleasure. I'm glad I could be of assistance. I'll talk to you soon. Goodbye." His final words were still making their way to the back room when he entered the storage area.

Susan introduced the store's owner to her colleague. She kept the introduction brief, mainly because she didn't know much about Oliver. As she turned to Bill to finish the second part of the ritual, she looked her colleague straight in the eye. He nearly stared a hole through her, indicating that he was ready to leave. Meeting his stare with a calm smile, Susan spared the details on Bill's bio and suggested that they get started.

Always the gracious host, Oliver offered his guests something to drink. Both declined. He picked up a white carafe from a table in the corner, poured water in a ceramic mug, and began to peruse the tea-bags stored in a wooden box. After several seconds passed, he selected one. "Yes, this will work just fine," he said to himself. He removed the teabag from its packaging and placed it in the hot water. As he walked to the table, he discarded the wrapper into a small trash can.

The portable table wobbled slightly as Oliver placed his mug in front of the third seat. He sat down and looked first at Susan, where he benefited from her ever-present smile, and then at Bill, who failed to provide a similar benefit.

Oliver wasn't shaken by Bill's demeanor.

"Okay," he said, "let's begin."

Chapter 6: Ground Rules

"I have to admit that I didn't think you'd come today," Oliver said to Susan. Turning to Bill, he added, "And I didn't expect you to bring someone with you. This is a pleasant surprise."

"Well, since we're coming clean on things, I must admit that I'm surprised I came as well. Don't get me wrong," she said with a bit of hesitation, "I'm not intending to be disrespectful. It's just we only briefly met. I'm not sure how you can really help, and I'm guarded about sharing much about our organization."

"That's fair enough," Oliver said. "Why don't we lay down some ground rules for our conversation? You're right, we know very little about each other. Perhaps we could agree to what should or shouldn't be shared." He paused to gather his thoughts. "I don't know about the two of you, but I often find that setting some professional boundaries can be helpful."

Susan and Bill shared a look of relief. "That sounds like a good idea," Bill responded. "What do you have in mind?"

"First, I see no need for the two of you to tell me specifics about your organization." As Oliver talked, the tension seemed to leave the room. "I don't need to know the details about what your employees do or how your organization is currently performing. In fact, I suggest that you convey only what you feel comfortable sharing. I imagine that we'll mostly discuss general ideas about organizations, how they perform, and what I've learned about improving performance. How does that sound?"

Susan's eyes brightened. "That sounds good," she responded. Bill nodded in agreement.

"Second, as Susan and I agreed to on the phone, let's meet for one hour today. There are no commitments or expectations beyond that. If the two of you find the conversation helpful, that's great, and we can get together again to continue. If you felt it was a waste of your time, no harm done. In fact, I recommend we make no commitments today about getting together again. You two can talk about it after you leave. Susan has my number."

Bill and Susan both agreed that this was a good approach. Susan added in her usual tone that they did value his time and expected that the session would be beneficial.

"Third, you might be concerned that you're committing your organization to some sort of consulting agreement and that I will hand you an invoice when you leave. Let me assure you, this is not the case. I'm not a consultant—I'm an avid reader. Consider this more of a book club." As Oliver explained ground rule three, he watched Bill's face light up. Again, his tablemates nodded in agreement. "I have one last ground rule." He looked at Susan first and then at Bill. His face conveyed complete sincerity. "I'm an open book," he said. "Ask me anything you like. My only goal for our time together is to help the two of you help your organization—nothing more."

Oliver's ability to put people at ease was evident. They both believed him.

Bill and Susan indicated that the ground rules seemed sufficient. Their new teacher asked a few general questions about their organization. He inquired about their industry, the size of their teams, and about how long each of them had worked there. Staying true to the ground rules, he didn't ask any specifics about the type of work they did or how they went about doing it.

Susan took the lead. She explained that they worked for a government organization with about 350 employees providing IT services to several other government entities. According to Susan, most people simply referred to the organization as "the agency." Yes, it had a specific name that had been reduced to an acronym, but they had gone through several organizational changes in the last decade. With every reorganization came a new name, a new acronym, and new letterhead. To maintain sanity and some sense of continuity, most people within the organization simply called it "the agency."

When she finished her brief overview, Oliver walked to the chalkboard, cleared his throat, and rolled up his sleeves. He turned to Bill and Susan and began to teach. "The other day when Susan visited the store, she asked me about books on performance improvement. As I explained to her, we have lots of books on performance improvement. Every year many texts hit the market that deal with various aspects of improvement. Just take a look at the stacks I assembled this morning." He pointed to several and paused for dramatic effect. "These stacks represent what various authors have written about the subject from a number of different viewpoints. Whether writing from the perspective of general management, leadership, statistics, marketing, or a wide range of other functions, they collectively make the argument for a number of steps that leaders and their teams should follow to be most successful."

"Five of them, right?" Susan added.

"Yes, I believe the ideas distill down to five essential steps. Over the years, I have shared these five steps with many people. Some were leaders in large organizations, like the two of you; others were people who worked in the smallest of teams. Not only do these leaders agree with me when I explain the steps to them, but I have heard some amazing stories of the results they achieved by applying these steps."

He turned and picked up a piece of chalk sitting in the small trough at the base of the chalkboard. The board appeared to be decades old and was framed by a border of dark wood that rested on two sturdy legs. The legs sat on caster wheels, and although it had the ability to move, it appeared to have been positioned in the same place for years. On the left and right sides of the frame were two brass knobs, which could be loosened so the entire board would rotate, revealing the other side and, no doubt, more writing space. The chalkboard reminded Susan of her childhood. Her fourth grade teacher had had an identical board. Susan thought that if Ms. Ryan were still teaching today, she and Oliver would be the two people still using these chalkboard relics.

Oliver interrupted her daydream. "Ever since I was a kid, I've consistently done two things. First, I asked lots of questions, so much so that I drove my parents, teachers, and friends crazy. Second, I read everything and anything I could get my hands on. These two obsessions served me well in school and in business."

Susan and Bill glanced around the place.

Oliver watched as the two looked about. "Now I know what you're thinking." He looked pointedly at the mess surrounding them. "How did all this question asking and reading serve *him* well in business?" Without hesitation, he answered his own question. "Prior to purchasing this store some ten years ago, I owned a regional chain of bookstores called AC's."

Bill jumped in. "I'm familiar with that name. There were a couple of them here in town. I also think there were some upstate."

"Actually, just prior to selling them, there were three throughout this city and fifty-four stores in total," Oliver explained. "Things were going great and the business was thriving. Then one day I received a phone call on behalf of a national competitor. They asked if I was interested in selling. At first I said no, but they eventually put an offer on the table that I couldn't refuse." His smile revealed that the offer must have been quite sizeable. "After the deal went through, I hung around for about six months to help with the transition. Then I decided to try my hand at retirement. It didn't take. I started hanging around this place a lot and eventually made an offer to buy this store. In many ways, I'm back where I started. It's a different store in a different part of town, but I'm the same guy surrounded by books again."

Before Bill or Susan could add anything, Oliver turned to the chalkboard, drew a circle in the middle of it, and wrote the words "Your Team."

Oliver turned to face Bill and Susan and continued. "Let's begin with a brief discussion about the implementation of strategic plans. Of course, the execution of a strategy can break down for a number of reasons. Perhaps the strategy is not well thought out, so no matter how well implemented, the desired results will not be achieved. Other times, as the organization begins to implement a strategy, a major shift occurs that causes senior leadership to move in a different direction and discard or significantly revise the plan."

Bill and Susan both nodded their heads, suggesting that they had seen each of these situations play out in the past.

"However," Oliver continued, "from my experience, most strategies succeed or fail based on the decisions that teams and their leaders make every day. This happens because teams choose on a day-to-day basis how to apply the organization's resources. In doing so, they may elect to behave in ways that align with the strategy or run in opposition to it. Let's face it, at some point the grand strategy eventually lands on a team's shoulders, and it's their job to implement it. The *best* organizations are separated from the merely *good* ones not by their ability to plan, but by their ability to implement the plan. Successful implementation of a plan happens—or doesn't happen—at the team level.

"Is it fair to say that both of you lead teams and that your organization is made of teams, whether they be groups of three, ten, or fifty?"

Susan confirmed Oliver's suspicions. "Yes, our organization is made of teams. Some, like mine, are small with only a few employees, while others are much larger."

"Wonderful, that's what I suspected," Oliver responded as he turned again to face the board. He drew a second, much larger circle, around his original circle. This circle was made of dashed lines with the words "STEP 1: GAIN PERSPECTIVE" neatly printed at the top.

Oliver glanced over his shoulder and observed both Susan and Bill copying his illustration in their notes. Poised to explain step one, Oliver waited for them to finish their sketches. When both had completed the task, they looked first at one another and then at their teacher. With that, the lesson of their professional lifetime began.

Chapter 7: Begin at the Beginning

After neatly drawing the dashed circle and labeling it "STEP 1: GAIN PERSPECTIVE" on the chalkboard, Oliver explained the importance of perspective. He informed them that many books on organizational performance begin with some notion of understanding what is going on inside or outside the organization that will directly or indirectly affect a team's ability to implement the strategy. He emphasized terms that both of them recognized, such as Strengths, Weaknesses, Opportunities, and Threats Analysis, or SWOT, and 360-degree organizational assessments. He further explained two things that caught the attention of his participants. First, very few books deal directly with the challenges faced by public sector organizations. Second, even if they were to address government organizations, they would likely fail to provide detailed specifics that leaders could actually employ to meet the demands of their current situation.

As Oliver talked, both Bill and Susan were amazed by his ability to adapt to the situation. It had only been a few minutes since he had learned that they worked for a government organization. Nonetheless, he had modified his language and approach to connect directly to the challenges they faced in their roles. Not only did he start to use words they felt comfortable with, but he also hit on an issue that they both found frustrating.

Over their careers, each of them had invested countless hours reading books and attending workshops where the authors and speakers failed to deliver messages in a way that connected with the realities of what they experienced in their roles. In these previous learning experiences, Susan and Bill found that interesting ideas or concepts were typically discussed in the context of goals such as increasing revenues or improving net income. When this occurred, they believed that the value of the teaching was, at times, lost in translation as they attempted to connect commercial business language to the world of the government. However, they could tell that Oliver's approach was different. He got it.

"Perspective is all about determining what matters to those who matter to you. It helps you understand how things are currently performing, what is possible, and what is simply not going to happen. When you work in a large institution, such as the government, some things are within your control; however, many things are not. Gaining perspective on things affords you and your people the opportunity to put your best efforts and resources in action against things that really matter."

"Hold on," Bill interjected. "I have to stop you there. What about all of the things I've read and heard about setting grandiose goals and objectives? Aren't we, as leaders, supposed to be visionary?"

"Don't get me wrong," Oliver responded. "I'm not saying to squash creativity and initiative by *not* dreaming big. I'm saying that before you go charging down a new path, put things into perspective. There may very well be times in your career where you can set lofty goals to take your division in a new direction. There are also times where the goals are essentially dictated down to you, and your wisest move is to act on those goals first, deliver the results, and earn the right to take on the next challenge. Setting a grandiose goal or objective for your team might be exactly the right thing to do. I'm simply saying to pause first and assess the situation. In your world, grand plans without funding and senior leadership support are hallucinations. Perspective helps you determine what's possible and important today based upon current realities."

"Okay," Bill replied. "You aren't saying dream small, you're saying dream smart."

"Exactly!"

"Well, how do we do that?" retorted Bill.

"That's precisely what we're going to discuss next. We'll use a tool I call the *Perspective Matrix.*" Oliver turned to the board and wrote four words: *Who, What, How,* and *Which.* Underneath each, he wrote a question.

Perspective Matrix

WHO	WHAT
Who do we serve?	What matters most to them?
HOW	**WHICH**
How are they doing at what matters most to them?	Which areas that matter most can our team impact?

"I know these are simple questions, but the answers are critical. The first focuses on who we serve. All too often, teams think they exist simply because the organizational structure dictates their existence. They have a box on the organizational chart. They are in the staffing documents. Therefore, they have a rightful seat at the table. Although this is true to an extent, all organizations, divisions, teams, and individual employees exist to serve others."

Susan stopped taking notes and looked up from her paper. Her eyes looked toward the ceiling and her head tilted slightly to the right. Oliver sensed her concern and paused.

"If we were the corner coffee shop that might be easy to answer, but in our world, things are more complicated. I have all sorts of people that I serve. I have my direct boss, and I have the other leaders in the agency. I also have individual team members who rely on our office for a number of issues, and I answer to other HR people in other agencies who dictate what we can and can't do. On top of that, we get put on ad hoc teams inside and outside the agency that place demands on our time."

Bill added a short, "Ditto," and the ball was back in Oliver's court.

"Fair enough—I suggest you invest some time developing a complete customer list. You can prioritize them later, but for now, just capture all of them." Susan and Bill nodded, and Oliver returned to the chalkboard. "Once you have listed your *whos*, now consider what matters most to them. In some instances, answering this question can be achieved by reading through some documentation. If your boss just generated a plan for the future, read it to see what matters. In most cases, though, answering this question requires an actual face-to-face conversation."

Susan and Bill both saw the humor in the statement. Other than a formal staff meeting or a quick conversation in the hallway, neither could think of a real conversation in last the several weeks with anyone who might appear on their list.

"You can phrase things any way you'd like. What you are trying to find out from each person is what matters most to him or her." Oliver smiled wryly, "You will have to trust me on this one, but I think you'll be surprised to find that many people haven't thought through their answer to this question."

"I'm sure our boss's boss has," Susan added. "Remember, we have twenty-four different metrics that he measures and we talk about every week at our staff meetings."

"Yes, I remember." Oliver reflected back on his first conversation with Susan. "But I would suggest that we're confusing a couple of different things here. In most organizations, we tend to measure what can be measured without truly thinking through what's most important. Consider my bookstore. I can measure all sorts of things: how many customers come in every day; how many books I have in stock; how many items each customer purchases; how many times I'm asked for something that is out of stock; how many times I'm asked for something that is in stock; how many people call every day with questions; how quickly I answer the phone when they call. The list could go on and on. The key isn't measuring everything. The key is sorting through all the possible measures and culling out the ones that if focused on and improved really make all the difference in the world.

"Here's my challenge to both of you. Go back to your office, talk to your teams, talk to those who matter most to your teams, and try to answer the questions for the top three customers you support. Second, seize the opportunity the next time the twenty-four measures are discussed to ask the question, 'Of all these measures, which ones really matter most?' You can fully expect at first that you will be told that each one matters most. I encourage you not to accept the initial response as the final answer. Push back a little bit by saying something like, 'Okay, I imagine they are all important—otherwise we wouldn't be talking about them. But if you had to identify the few critical ones, which would they be?'"

Surprisingly, Bill responded first with a hearty, "You know what, Oliver? We've got nothing to lose. I'll commit to doing both of the things you asked and to coming back here next week if you're willing to discuss how things are progressing."

Susan added that she would do the same. They wrapped up their discussion as they walked out of the back room and through the store. Trailing behind them Oliver called out, "I look forward to hearing how things go. Let's plan on getting together the same time next week. After we discuss how things are progressing, I'll share the second step with you."

As they walked out the door, both turned and smiled at Oliver. Susan mouthed a quick, "Thank you" to him as they stepped into the afternoon sun.

Chapter 8: Gaining Perspective

As they drove back to the office, Susan and Bill talked about the session with Oliver. They both agreed that they would spend some time on their own over the next day working to answer the questions he had outlined for them. Both felt that they could take a fairly good stab at answering the questions for those individuals or teams that they felt represented the top three most important customers. They also agreed that they would get together prior to the next Monday morning staff meeting, share their progress with each other, and decide how they would tackle asking questions about Mr. Morgan's twenty-four metrics.

Friday morning arrived early for Susan. She was up well before dawn and was the first person in the office. Despite her initial reservations about answering Oliver's questions, she found the process invigorating. She started by creating an exhaustive list of all the people who mattered to her team. Admittedly, had she answered the question, "Who matters to your team?" off the cuff, she probably would have replied that there are only a handful of people or teams that mattered. However, after ten minutes of pondering the question, she had a fairly exhaustive list of over thirty individuals or teams that mattered. *Now the hard part*, she thought. Somehow, she had to narrow the list down to the few that mattered most. Her first pass through the list quickly cut it to less than fifteen names. A second time through and she was down to eight. *Eight isn't bad*, she thought, *but it's a far cry from three, and Bill and I agreed to three*. Then she remembered something Oliver said.

He mentioned that when prioritizing, you have to separate the merely important from those that matter most.

She looked down at the list of eight names and said to herself, "Okay, Susan, if my team failed to deliver on our responsibilities to three teams or individuals on this list, which ones would have the biggest impact on our future?" The answer jumped out at her. She crossed out five names, leaving herself with the name of Sam Finch (her boss), Mel Taylor (the operations manager), and the name of an outside team she was supporting. Leaving Sam's name on the list made sense. She figured if the boss wasn't happy, nothing else mattered too much. She added Mel's team because he was understaffed and faced several HR-related challenges. Lastly, she included a team outside the agency where she was working to help restructure several HR policies that would influence both her agency and other federal organizations. The powers that be called the team IMPROVE. It stood for Internal Management, Policy Review, and OVersight Enhancement. When she first saw the name, Susan chuckled to herself, thinking, *It isn't a real project team if it doesn't have a catchy acronym.*

She set out to identify what mattered most to each of them. She started with Sam and listed a number of things that she felt were important to him. Some were items that she had heard him talk about numerous times. Others were assumptions that she had made based on what had mattered to past directors. The list was becoming fairly lengthy, and as she tried to assess current performance, she began to realize that there were a lot of blanks on the page. She decided to transition to Mel's team and quickly found herself in a similar predicament. Susan then turned her attention to the IMPROVE team. She found this one to be a bit easier to address. The team was fairly new, but they had developed some initial project outcomes they were looking to achieve. So, listing what mattered most was easy. Identifying current performance was quickly accomplished too since other than establishing their initial charter, they had really failed to accomplish anything of value to date.

Staring down at a piece of paper peppered with names, some sketchy assumptions, and plenty of blank spaces, Susan decided her next step was to talk to Mel. She figured she could wait to talk to Sam until after the Monday morning staff meeting and his subsequent weekly discussion with Mr. Morgan. As for the IMPROVE team, that might need to wait a bit longer until she had a chance to sit down and talk to the team's chairperson, who, frankly, was out of her office on business travel more often than not.

That afternoon, she managed to catch up with Mel. Susan and Mel spent the better part of an hour together. At first he was distracted, and his ever-present red face suggested the stress he was under. After five minutes or so, though, the conversation became very productive.

Susan started the discussion simply by saying, "Mel, I'm trying to help my team focus its energy on what truly matters most. To do so, I listed a number of customers that we serve both inside and outside the agency and then narrowed it down to the few that seem to be the highest priority at the moment. Your team landed on the short list, and I was hoping to spend some time together making sure I understand your priorities." She added a warm smile conveying her sincerity.

Mel responded enthusiastically to her inquiry. He looked at the list of issues she had identified for his team. He confirmed most, deleted a few, and added a couple. He then assessed how his team was performing in each area and helped her think through where the HR team might be able to provide some support. In the end, they came up with four or five areas where the HR team might be able to provide both short- and long-term assistance.

As she walked out of Mel's office, he stopped her and said, "You know, Susan, the last thing I like to do on a Friday afternoon is add another meeting to the calendar, but I'm sure glad you stopped by to talk. I've been up nights trying to figure out some of the performance issues we're facing and never seem to get to the staffing and training challenges. I'm glad we took the time to discuss them. I know we didn't solve anything specifically, but I feel like we might be on our way."

Susan replied, "Mel, I should thank you. I appreciate you helping me better understand the challenges you guys are facing. It really helps me to put things into perspective." The word "perspective" had barely left her mouth before she found herself smiling a bit. At the same time, she swore to herself that Mel's ever-red face had lightened a few shades over the course of their conversation.

First thing Monday morning, Susan was sitting at her desk reflecting on her conversation with Mel the previous Friday. Bill Engleman arrived at her door. "Boy, you're in early this morning. Are you scrambling to get your perspective homework completed?"

Bill's question brought her back to the present. She spun around in her desk chair and responded to his inquiry. "To be honest, I didn't get all of my homework done, but I did make some really good progress. I'm excited to compare notes about what I've learned so far."

In his typical fashion, Bill responded with a somewhat cynical, "Well, I would say that I'm excited to share what I learned. But frankly, until my second or third cup of coffee, I barely get above disinterested on a Monday morning. I *did* learn some interesting things over the last couple of days, and I want to hear how things went for you." He glanced at his watch to check the time, and realizing he only had a few minutes, he excused himself, saying, "Susan, let me run to my office, drop off a few things, grab my perspective notes and a cup of coffee, and meet you back here in ten minutes."

Before she could respond, he was gone.

As promised, Bill was back in ten minutes, and the two sat down at a small table in the corner of her office to share their work. Susan went first and described her approach to identifying her team's customers and then narrowing the list to the top three. She discussed her challenges with filling in the form and her decision to meet with Mel in person. Susan emphasized the value of the conversation, and Bill even seemed to smile when she mentioned that Mel's face had appeared to lighten by the end of the discussion.

When it was Bill's turn, his explanation was less descriptive than Susan's, but it was clear that he had made some great progress. He too had narrowed his customer list to three. Like Susan's list, Bill's included Sam, the interim director. As with Susan, Bill had decided to wait until after the Monday morning staff meeting to approach Sam. They immediately agreed that they would approach Sam together later that day, after he had met with Mr. Morgan. Bill continued with his client list. He had identified two divisions within the agency that required attention because of the specific ramifications their current actions had on the budgeting process. Like Susan, Bill had seized the initiative to talk to each of the two division leaders and had used the discussion to complete his *Perspective Matrix*.

Both were pleased with their progress and agreed that the process of putting things in perspective was valuable.

The discussion turned to how best to approach the Monday morning staff meeting. Although Bill was a bit hesitant to come right out and ask Oliver's question to Jane Hudson, Susan expressed that she was willing to address the issue straight on with Mr. Morgan's surrogate and let the chips fall where they may. She added, "Bill, we go in there every week and get beat up by Jane. What's the worst that can happen if I ask a question or two?"

The comment had barely emerged from Susan's mouth when a reminder popped up on her computer screen along with a chime to catch her attention. "Well, we're about to find out," Susan said. "The meeting starts in five minutes. We need to get going." The two of them sprang to their feet and headed to the conference room.

Chapter 9: Staff Meeting with a Twist

As was the normal routine, the leadership team filed into the meeting room and took their seats. Susan's mug rested in its usual position, and once again, the usual conversation about the weekend ensued. This time, however, Bill and Susan were clearly absent from the discussion. Instead, they were focused on the task at hand. Their job was to use Oliver's suggestions to challenge Jane Hudson, Mr. Morgan's surrogate, about the twenty-four metrics and identify which ones mattered most. The meeting continued as usual until it was Jane's turn to present. The chart with Mr. Morgan's metrics appeared on the screen. As she worked her way to the front of the room, everyone silently sat waiting for the weekly thrashing. Jane had barely begun her presentation when Susan interrupted. "Excuse me, Jane," she said. "May I ask a quick question before you get too far into your report?"

Jane turned toward the voice. The room was silent for a moment, not because of any particular tension, but simply because all were surprised that someone actually had a question. Frankly, the team had an unspoken agreement about the metrics discussion. Jane produced the latest results and shared Mr. Morgan's disappointment in their lack of progress. The leaders remained quiet, took their dose of weekly feedback, and got out of the room as quickly as possible. What was Susan thinking, breaking protocol? Any question asked was only going to slow down the process and make the pain last longer.

Jane was as shocked as the rest of them. "Please go ahead," she replied.

Susan cleared her throat, sat up a bit straighter in her chair, and began. "I've been thinking about the metrics we review each week. If you had to identify those that were *most* important to Mr. Morgan, which ones would they be?"

Just as Oliver predicted, Jane responded, "Well, they're all important. If they weren't important, Mr. Morgan wouldn't have asked us to track them."

Following Oliver's suggestion, Jane replied, "Oh, I didn't mean to suggest that they weren't all important. I'm just curious if you could name the top few. You know, the three or so that matter most at this moment, what would they be?"

Surprisingly, Jane had an answer. Without hesitation, she said, "Okay, I see what you're asking, and frankly had you asked that question last week, I probably wouldn't have had a good answer for you. However, late last week, I met with Mr. Morgan to discuss the beginning of a strategic planning effort he's about to start. In the discussion, he identified his top four objectives, or pillars, as he calls them. Please keep in mind that these aren't solidified and will likely change some as they are refined; however, since you asked, I'm willing to share. I don't think Mr. Morgan will take issue with my sharing his preliminary ideas with you in an effort to answer your question."

In an instant, two things changed in the room. First, in the group's eyes, Jane moved from Mr. Morgan's minion to someone who appeared to be even a bit on their side. Second, instead of wanting to run for the door, the entire leadership team was anxious to hear what Jane had to say.

"Let me pull up a presentation I'm working on that captures the essence of my discussion with Mr. Morgan." Jane purposefully walked over to her laptop, which was connected to the projector in the back of the room, to search for the file. As she looked for it, Jane thought that Mr. Morgan may very much care that she was sharing the information with the agency. In fact, he hadn't even seen, much less approved, the materials she was about to share. But in that instant, Jane was concerned less about possibly upsetting her boss than she was about helping the agency's leadership. It was her hope from the start that she would be able to help them win on the metrics. This was her first and perhaps only chance, and she wasn't going to let it pass.

"Yes, here it is." Jane motioned toward the screen. On it appeared a slide that read, "Preliminary Strategic Direction." "Again, I should include the caveat that this is a draft and hasn't been fully vetted by Mr. Morgan, so please keep the information to yourselves. In the coming weeks, he will refine these thoughts as he prepares for a strategic planning session that will take place in the early summer."

Glancing at his calendar, Sam added, "Yes, I believe the session is scheduled for three days in mid-April. I've been asked to be there; however, other than putting the dates on my calendar, I have little insight into what we're going to be doing."

"My understanding," Jane responded, "is that you and Mr. Morgan's other direct reports will be going through a planning session focused on the development of a three- to five-year strategic plan. The discussion will include reviewing the results of an internal and external assessment that is underway and the creation of strategic goals and objectives that build on Mr. Morgan's preliminary strategic direction." Jane clicked the remote to reveal the second slide, which displayed the words "Pillar One: Operational Excellence."

What transpired from the time Jane put up the "Pillar One" slide until Sam made his adjournment announcement amazed Susan and Bill. They watched Jane explain Mr. Morgan's four pillars of success. In addition to the operational excellence pillar, pillars two through four focused on financial stewardship, policy, and people development. The dialogue was robust. The team members were energized and began to see how the twenty-four metrics tied or, in some cases, *didn't* tie to the newly stated priorities. Suddenly, the complex metrics began to make sense to the leaders.

At one point, Michael Thomas, the former basketball player and current chief of Plans and Policy, grabbed a flipchart and started capturing items on the paper. He looked like a basketball coach sketching out the final play for the win at the buzzer as he drew lines connecting the twenty-four metrics to the four pillars. From the time Susan asked her question, the meeting continued for another hour, ending only when Sam stood up and said he had to run in order to get ready for his session with Mr. Morgan. Had it not been for that announcement, the conversation would have continued.

Sam departed, but an informal discussion continued for a few minutes longer until one by one the leaders filed out of the room and only three people remained. Bill and Susan stood by the door briefly chatting about what had just happened while Jane packed up her computer and shut down the projector. They had yet to leave the room when Jane completed her task and caught up with them. "Well, that was an interesting discussion," Jane said.

"Yes, it was," Bill responded with enthusiasm.

"I have to admit," Jane added, "I'm glad you asked your question." This was the first time Susan had seen Jane smile.

"So am I," replied Susan.

With that, the three of them said their goodbyes and headed out the door.

★ ★ ★

Two nights later, Susan and her husband Greg enjoyed a quiet dinner at home. Greg had been out of town since early Monday morning, and the two were glad to be back together. Susan found Greg to be a great listener and advisor when it came to thinking through the challenges she faced at work.

They finished the meal, cleared the dinner table, and began to clean up the kitchen. As they worked together to wash the dishes, Susan shared with Greg the events of the week. She picked up where their conversation had last ended with the two of them rushing out the door Monday morning prior to her meeting with Bill. She shared with him her discussion with Bill and how her question at the Monday morning staff meeting started a much-needed conversation among the leadership team. She also filled him in on the conversation she had the following day with Sam about his goals and how her team could help him achieve them.

"Did you tell him about Oliver and show him the *Perspective Matrix*?" Greg asked.

"No, I decided to hold off on that conversation until I had another chance to meet with Oliver and perhaps got a bit further into the learning."

"What made you decide to hold off on telling Sam?"

"I *do* feel that we can learn a lot from Oliver, but I don't want to get Sam's hopes up. I'd rather wait to see where things go and bring Sam up to speed when the timing seems right."

Step 1: Gain Perspecitve

"Perspective is all about determining what matters to those who matter to you."

KEY POINTS:

Grand plans without funding and senior leadership support are hallucinations.

All organizations, divisions, teams, and individual employees exist to serve others.

Don't simply measure what can be measured, measure what is important.

Customers are often pleasantly surprised when you ask them what matters most to them.

Great questions generate great conversations.

LEADER CHECKLIST:

✔ Brainstorm list of customers

✔ Identify your top three customers

✔ Complete the Perspective Matrix Tool by answering the following:
- Who do we serve?
- What matters most to them?
- How are they performing on what matters most to them?
- Which areas that matter most can our team impact?

Step 2: Define Purpose

Chapter 10: New Student

When the Thursday morning meeting time arrived at Oliver's Spot, the store's owner was surprised to see that a third student had joined the class. After the staff meeting, Michael Thomas had stopped by Susan's office to talk about the discussion and to inquire as to what had motivated her to ask Jane the question. Susan told Michael about the previous week's meeting that she and Bill had had with Oliver and of what they'd learned. Susan was shocked when Michael nearly insisted that he attend the next session. With that, the group of two grew to three, and Michael found himself wedged into a seat in Oliver's back room. Unlike the other students who seemed relatively comfortable in the surroundings, Michael was crammed into his space at the table. Nonetheless, he was seated and ready to start when Oliver made his way into the room. To Susan, Michael looked like an adult sitting at the kid's table.

"Before we start the next step, I'm curious how things went this past week. Were you able to look into the issue of perspective?" Oliver asked.

Bill and Susan provided Oliver a quick update of the week's events. They explained the progress they had made and some of the challenges they'd encountered. When the discussion turned to the weekly staff meeting, Michael added to the conversation by sharing that Susan's question about the twenty-four metrics truly ignited the leaders with an energy he had yet to see since Mr. Morgan sent Jane Hudson to monitor performance. Michael stated, "At one point, it even felt like Jane was on our team, helping us to figure out what truly mattered to Mr. Morgan. I for one started to see what really matters to those above our boss. The complex metrics began to make sense to us."

Oliver was pleased with their progress, and after a ten-minute recap of the week's events, he worked his way to the old chalkboard. A dusty piece of chalk in one hand, Oliver erased the words "Your Team" from the middle circle and replaced them with "STEP 2: DEFINE PURPOSE."

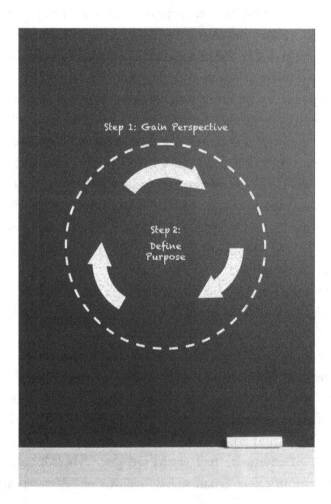

Oliver ran his hand through his hair, turned to face the team, and began his lesson. "I recognize that each of you has some work to accomplish in order to gain a true perspective, but you've made some great strides, and I trust you'll continue your efforts." He made his way to the open seat at the table and said, "The second step is about defining the purpose for your team. That's articulating why your team exists, what you do, and who you serve—"

Michael interrupted, "Oliver, I have a quick question. Excuse me if I'm off base, but don't people already know why my team exists? After all, our directorate's title is pretty clear."

"That's a fair question," Oliver responded. "Now, most people think that everyone, both inside and outside the team, knows their team's purpose. After all, the team is listed on the organization chart, and as you said, the title of the team often conveys what the team does."

He paused for a moment to gather his thoughts before he continued. "Michael, let's take your team as an example. You said that you are in charge of plans and policy. Is that correct?"

Michael nodded his head and responded with a short, "Yes."

"Would you agree or disagree that there have been times in the past when people have misunderstood the purpose of your team? This might have occurred when they expected your team to do something you believed was outside the scope of your team's role or if they criticized your team for not accomplishing something that, in fact, you had little or no control over."

Now Oliver had Michael's attention. He sat up even straighter in his chair, making his already large frame appear bigger, and responded with a strong, "Yes, that happens all too often."

Oliver continued, "This type of situation occurs for a number of reasons. Sometimes it's simply people trying to get you and your teams to accomplish something they don't want to do. Other times, it's a new task that has no clear home within the organization and by default ends up on your team's plate. However, more often than not, people simply *aren't clear* on the purpose of your team. In my years of studying the subject and personal experience, I have observed that, left to their own devices, people will define your team to be *whatever* they want it to be. This can be a very dangerous situation. It can lead to all sorts of communication and performance breakdowns. These breakdowns are often the result of a lack of shared expectations. Clarifying your team's purpose is all about creating shared expectations both inside and outside your team."

Oliver observed the group's reaction. From the looks on their faces, all three seemed to agree with his comments. "Just between the four of us, on a scale of one to five, with one being low and five being high, how well would your team members agree with these three statements? First, what score would your team members give to the statement, 'My team has a clearly defined purpose'?"

Oliver paused while everyone gathered their thoughts. Then he went around the table to get a sense of where each person stood. Sitting to Oliver's immediate left was Susan, and she admitted that she might struggle herself with clearly articulating her team's precise purpose, and she imagined her team would do the same. She scored her team a three. Next was Bill. A man of few words, he simply said that his team was a four. Michael agreed with Bill's assessment and gave his team a four as well.

After going around the table, Oliver provided the second statement. "How well would your people score the statement, 'My team members know our team's purpose'?"

Another pass around the table revealed two three and a halves and one three.

"Now, the last statement," Oliver said. "Using the same one-to-five scale, how would your team members score the statement, 'Our stakeholders know our team's purpose'?" He wasn't surprised when all three ranked their teams below three on the one-to-five scale. "I applaud your honesty," Oliver said. "The reality is that most teams don't do the hard work of communicating their purpose and rarely take the time to assess how well everyone knows the team's purpose within and outside the team."

Although quiet for most of the discussion, Bill took the pause in the conversation to add his thoughts. "I must admit, I had never really given this issue much consideration. I guess I always figured that people knew what my office does, but I'm often surprised at how few people can distinguish the various roles we perform. In fact, my experience suggests that most people can't tell me the difference between accounting and budgeting. The reality is that it's all money to them, and as long as I help them get what they need, they're fine with me. If they don't like what I tell them, they just go around me." Susan and Michael both chuckled at this assessment. "I do think it would be beneficial if everyone was clear on what my team does," Bill added.

"Bill's right," Susan said. "We run into the same problem. My question is, if defining the purpose of the team is so important, how does a team go about doing it? Is it something that I create and share with them, or do we do it together?"

"That's a great question," Oliver responded. "I have found, and the books I have on my shelves suggest, that the best way to define the team's purpose is for the leader to draft a statement, two or three sentences in length, and then share it with the team for them to provide feedback and to put their own touch on the purpose statement."

"Okay, that makes sense," Susan added. "So what goes into a good purpose statement?"

"Another great question," Oliver said. "Team purpose statements focus on why the work of the team matters. They help team members and external stakeholders understand how the team connects to what matters most to the organization and define what customer needs the team addresses. Teams that explain these items in a few sentences and ensure that every team member can explain the team's purpose statement are in a far better place than teams that can't.

"My suggestion to each of you is that you reflect on the purpose of your team, couple that with the information you gathered during the perspective step, and draft a statement. I've found that it takes a leader some time to draft the statement and then about an hour or so to review it with his or her team to get feedback. Any more time spent than that becomes an argument over using the word 'happy' versus 'glad.' Let's face it, trying to write a few sentences by committee can be painful. Just get your team's input based on your initial attempt at the statement. Then take all of their thoughts under consideration and finalize the statement. If you'd like, you can float the revised version past everyone one more time for comments before you go final."

"That sounds like a pretty good plan," Susan replied. "But what do we do with the perspective information we have developed so far?" She rested her chin on her hands with her elbows on the table.

"What do you think?" Oliver asked.

"I guess we share it with them to help them better see what's going on. I know that clarity helped me; it would probably be useful to them as well."

"Certainly," Oliver confirmed. "That's exactly what you need to do. I do have one last thought. You and Bill made great progress in one week with the perspective piece. I'm sure Michael will work hard to catch up with the two of you. Keep the momentum. Draft your statements today, if possible, and meet with your teams in the next few days. Teams that do well at implementing the five steps have a bias for action."

The three agreed that they would follow the same schedule Bill and Susan established last week. They would work to draft their purpose statements and talk to their teams and then get together Monday morning before the staff meeting to discuss their progress. They also agreed to meet with Oliver the following Thursday morning to discuss progress and to learn about step three.

Chapter 11: Bringing the Team on Board

Susan took Oliver's suggestion and set up a meeting for early Friday afternoon with her three direct reports. Before the meeting, she didn't give many details but simply explained that she wanted to spend some time together talking about the direction of the HR directorate and do a little team building. With only minor resistance, each agreed that they could move a few things around on their calendars to make the short-notice meeting happen.

All three respected Susan as a leader. Two of them, Kimberly and Chris, rarely second-guessed Susan's decisions. The third, Todd, seemed to push back on any and all requests he received from her or anyone else. Susan knew that he was competent in his role, but she had concerns about his attitude. She felt that if they were going to really advance as a team, Todd would need to be addressed. At the time, she didn't realize that the five steps Oliver was taking her through would have such a dramatic impact on Todd's attitude and performance.

After setting up the meeting with her team, Susan spent an hour late Thursday afternoon and another one that evening working on a draft purpose statement. Her husband, Greg, helped her put the finishing touches on it. Susan and Greg had been married for almost twenty years, and she always trusted his advice and counsel. As she got ready for bed, she felt good about what she had accomplished so far and looked forward to sharing with her team and gaining their input.

Friday morning quickly passed. When she arrived at work, two urgent voicemails awaited her, and she worked until noon putting out the proverbial fires that creep up in the workplace. She was barely able to print out copies of the draft statement before meeting with her team.

When she arrived, all three of her team members were present. She grabbed the fourth and final chair in the conference room and pulled it up to the table. Susan and her team members had worked together for the better part of the last three years. They had grown close and, for the most part, got along well with one another. Reflecting earlier that morning on the closeness of her team, she had decided to start the meeting with a little exercise.

"Thanks for dropping everything and meeting with me on short notice," Susan started.

"Did we have a choice?" Todd added, somewhat sarcastically. He saw that his comment wasn't well received and offered a quick, "Just kidding."

Susan shot him a glance and continued. "I'm hoping that each of you will find the next hour very interesting." She looked around the table at her three direct reports. Chris sat to her left. He was in charge of the agency's training and development initiatives. Chris was young and energetic. In his late twenties, the agency was his first stop in what promised to be an outstanding career. Next was Kimberly. Kim, as everyone called her, was responsible for recruiting people into the agency, familiarizing them with the environment once they arrived, and handling retirements, transfers, and other issues associated with someone departing the agency. To Susan's immediate right was Todd. He ran the agency's award and recognition program, as well as a new initiative underway that focused on employee retention. Despite Todd's cynical nature, he appeared as eager as the others to hear what Susan had to say.

Susan passed out three blank pieces of paper. She explained the importance of a team purpose statement and told them that she had spent some time drafting one for the team; however, before she shared it with them, she wanted to see how they saw the HR team's purpose. She gave them fifteen minutes to draft a team purpose statement individually and asked that each of them be prepared to share their thoughts when the time expired. Susan kept track of the time, and everyone dove into their drafting.

When fifteen minutes had elapsed, Susan said with a grin, "Okay, time's up—pencils down please."

"What are we, back in school?" Todd joked.

Chris latched on to the humor. He looked down at his paper and added, "Based on what I wrote, I hope Susan is grading with a curve."

Everyone laughed.

Susan invited each person at the table to read what was written on their page. She was amazed at the differences in the three statements. While Chris's attempt was short and to the point, Todd's was much longer. He listed almost everything that the team did in every aspect of their roles. Kim's was somewhere in the middle in both length and detail. When all three finished reading, Susan passed out a copy of her take on their purpose statement. She admitted that she had taken longer than fifteen minutes to craft the statement, but she felt that their versions were as good as or better than what she'd put together.

Everyone took a moment to read Susan's attempt. Once they all had a chance to digest it, they launched into a conversation about how they might adjust Susan's example to include a few aspects of the other team members' versions. The next forty-five minutes flew by as they talked about, adjusted, and began to own their purpose statement. They then discussed how they could use the purpose statement to better explain to people their individual roles and how they function as a team to support the agency. Susan found the conversation invigorating. It was the most energy and passion she had heard from the team in a long while. She was most amazed at how Todd joined in the discussion. Sure, he cracked a joke or two, but much of the cynicism that had been present was not showing itself.

Wanting to avoid the concern Oliver mentioned about trying to write a sentence by committee, Susan looked for a pause in the discussion and brought the meeting to an end, saying, "I just looked at my watch and realized that we're over time. I appreciate everybody's efforts and input. How about I take all of this information and come up with one last version for each of you to review?"

"That sounds great!" Kim said. Her colleagues nodded in agreement.

"One last thing before we finish. I'd like us to get together again next Friday to talk a bit further about our team and to build on today's efforts. Once I have something, I'll send out the statement we drafted today for everyone's review. So let's plan for the same time next week."

★ ★ ★

Susan and her husband Greg took a much-needed getaway over the weekend. The demands of work created the need to reconnect. Normally work was off-limits on these types of trips, but Susan was so excited about the progress she was making with her team that Greg agreed that they would make an exception to listen to her talk about work. They did agree, however, to limit work discussions to their time in the car. Work was off-limits once they reached the hotel.

Staying true to the agreement, the agency, Oliver's teaching, and the progress she was making with her team were not discussed after arriving at their hotel. However, as the car worked its way north along the winding road, the conversation covered little but Susan's work-related topics.

Greg found himself particularly interested in what she had to say as he planned to apply what she was learning to his own team at work. They spent the drive up talking about what she had learned thus far and most of the drive back guessing what Oliver would teach the following Thursday. They figured that since *perspective* and *purpose* started with a P, there was a good chance that whatever the topic this week, step three would also start with a P. They were right.

Chapter 12: Progress Check

Five minutes before starting time, Susan and Michael were settled into their seats. Although the discussion hadn't officially had begun, Bill and Oliver were already engaged in deep conversation about how things were going with Bill's team. Susan listened as the two men exchanged thoughts. Her ability to focus on their discussion was hampered by her interest in watching Michael fold himself into his seat. After working his way into his chair, he apparently decided to remove his coat. For some reason, he elected to accomplish this without standing back up and moving to where there was more space for him to maneuver out of the jacket. Susan laughed aloud as she watched him struggle with his jacket and nearly break his hand as he banged it against the back wall. He hit the wall so hard that Bill and Oliver stopped their discussion for a moment to see if he was okay. He said he was fine, and the two continued. As he finally extracted himself from his coat, Michael caught Susan's eye and made a sheepish look.

Right on time, Oliver brought his conversation with Bill to a close and began the session. "All right," Oliver said, "I've had a bit of an update from Bill, and I'm encouraged by how things went with his team. I'm curious to see how things progressed for the two of you."

Michael responded, "I have to admit that I didn't cover as much ground as I'd hoped." Oliver listened intently as Michael continued. "Perhaps I had expected too much, but I had a hard time getting both *perspective* and *purpose* accomplished this week. Frankly, the problem wasn't with covering the two steps as much as it was with getting the right people together to have the discussion."

Bill and Susan nodded in agreement.

"We're right in the middle of a major initiative. Three of my team members had to drop everything and take a quick trip to attend to some pretty big issues. So I was without a few key people for our discussion. I really want to get their input before I finalize anything."

When Michael paused to catch his breath, Susan jumped in. "Plus, early Monday morning we learned that our staff meeting was canceled as our boss, Sam, received notice of a last-minute meeting with his boss. Getting ready for the meeting required all of us to jump through hoops to pull reports together. So not only were we unable to learn more about the agency's metrics, none of us three had time to share our progress with one another."

Michael and Susan finished their updates, and Oliver responded to the situation. "You know, folks, I'm not at all surprised that you ran into some roadblocks this week. Day-to-day work often causes teams to have a hard time getting through the five steps. In fact, that's why so few of them do it. They either figure it is too hard to accomplish from the start, or they hit a bunch of scheduling conflicts and decide to give up before they really start to gain traction."

"Well, I'm not going to give up," said Susan. "The last few days have been tough, and I missed having our discussion Monday morning. But I'm optimistic about the progress my team has made thus far, despite the challenges of the day-to-day work."

"Go on," Oliver encouraged her. "Tell us more."

Susan explained how things had unfolded with her team. She shared how she'd drafted a team purpose, brought it to her team, had them create their own versions, and then worked together to craft a product. She also explained how she manipulated too much of her weekend with her husband talking about the progress and about how having the discussion about purpose had allowed her team to start feeling a collective sense of direction. She ended by saying, "I don't mean to be too dramatic, but I really felt that all three of my people, including the person who has been driving me a bit crazy lately, all seemed to enjoy the discussion."

"Susan, thanks for the update. Would you be willing to share the rest of the story?" Oliver asked.

"I'm not sure I know what you mean."

"May we hear your team purpose statement?"

Susan looked a bit surprised by the request. "Sure, I'll share, but I have to admit that it still needs some work. The latest version of the statement is currently with the team for feedback, and we're going to meet tomorrow to hopefully finalize it and get to work on step three."

She opened her binder and produced a piece of paper. The sheet was folded in half and tucked into a pocket inside the binder's front flap. Susan unfolded it, cleared her throat, and read from the paper: "The Human Resources team leads recruitment and on-boarding, provides training to the staff, and develops and sustains critical work-force development programs. We leverage our abilities to meet the demands of the agency's leaders and staff members. By providing them the skills, tools, and resources they need, they are freed up to focus on what matters most to the agency and our customers."

When she finished, Oliver, Bill, and Michael all applauded her efforts.

"That was great," Oliver said. "You should be very proud of your team's efforts. I think your write-up provides a clear picture of what your team does for the organization, who you do it for, and why it matters. I do have a couple of minor suggestions for you to consider."

Pen poised, Susan waited for his input.

"First, remember that less is more. You may want to remove any unnecessary words from the statement." He paused to look at the notes he'd jotted down as Susan had read her team's statement. "For example, as long as it doesn't lose the meaning of what you're trying to say, consider changing *provides training to the staff*, to *provides staff training*. It cuts out a couple of words and shortens the statement. Shorter statements are easier to remember."

Susan nodded in agreement. "That makes sense," she added.

Oliver continued, "I'd also suggest that you remove some of the jargon. You used the phrase *leverage our abilities to meet the demands*—that sounds like a lot of consultant double-talk. I'd just put it in plain English, saying something like *we work together to*. Well, those might not be the right words, so consider my thoughts here, not my words."

He paused while Susan finished her notes. When she was done writing, she looked up at him.

"Susan," Oliver continued, "let me be clear. These are just minor suggestions to help you with the language. The most important thing is that you and your team put a stake in the ground and proclaim, 'This is what we do, who we do it for, and why it matters.' That's big stuff, and I can see why you were so excited."

Susan smiled at Oliver and her colleagues.

Oliver then turned to Bill. "You gave me a pretty good rundown of how things went for you and your team this week. Why don't you share with the group, and if you don't mind, read us your team's purpose statement too."

Bill provided the group an update on his team's progress. Just like Susan, he had met with his team and crafted a purpose statement. He admitted that he wished he had tried Susan's approach because instead of giving them something to start with he simply brought his team into a room and had them work together to create a statement.

"It was like writing a sentence by committee and got pretty painful at times," he explained. "It took twice as long as I had planned, but we did get through it, and in the end everyone seemed pleased, although exhausted, with the result of our efforts."

With that, he shared his team's purpose statement. Oliver provided him feedback, and Bill committed to working with his team to finalize it over the next week. Michael also agreed to spend time with his team finishing steps one and two. Oliver suggested postponing the step three discussion for a week to allow all of them a chance to finish the first two steps. Surprisingly, all three of his students firmly declined his offer, suggesting that Oliver teach step three now and that they meet again in two weeks to share progress, agreeing that they would complete all three steps in that time.

Oliver agreed that the schedule made sense and launched into step three.

Step 2: Define Purpose

"Purpose is articulating why your team exists, what you do, and who you serve."

KEY POINTS:

More often than not, people inside and outside the team aren't always clear on the team's purpose.

Clarifying a team's purpose is about creating shared expectations.

Team purpose statements focus on why the work of the team matters.

If a team's purpose is not clearly understood, people will define it to be whatever they want it to be.

Great team purpose statements avoid unnecessary words and jargon. They are clear and concise.

LEADER CHECKLIST:

✔ Draft your team's purpose statement on your own

✔ Meet with the team and share your draft statement with them

✔ Solicit team member input and adjust the statement to best reflect your team's purpose

✔ Distribute the statement to those who matter to you and your team

✔ Use the statement daily as a reminder of who your team serves and why your work matters

Step 3: Determine Priorities

Chapter 13: Defining the What

"Susan is correct," Oliver began. "Step three does begin with the letter P. In fact, I'll go further and confirm that all five steps begin with the letter P. The third step focuses on defining your team's priorities."

Oliver paused as he watched Susan, Michael, and Bill jot down the word *priorities* in their notes. He then returned to his trusty chalkboard and added the words "STEP 3: DETERMINE PRIORITIES" to the graphic he'd started during the first session.

He waited for Susan, Bill, and Michael to add this to their graphic. When all three were ready, he said, "By priorities, I mean what are the key goals your team must accomplish to positively affect what matters most to those you serve, and to simultaneously impact your purpose. As you can see—" he pointed to the board "—determining priorities sits between the outer circle of perspective and the inner circle of purpose because your priorities are influenced by both. The challenge to step three is to identify these priorities."

Michael interjected, "I hear what you're saying, but the reality is that we have more things to work on—what you call priorities—than you can imagine. Every day we seem to have new items handed down to us that we must prioritize into our daily work. Now you want me to capture *all* those things we need to do?"

Oliver replied, "That's a great question. I'm not talking about coming up with an exhaustive list of all the work you and your people need to do and calling those your priorities. I'm talking about determining out of all the things you can do, which are most important. When I say most important, I mean those goals that will give the organization and the customers you serve the biggest bang for your buck, as the saying goes."

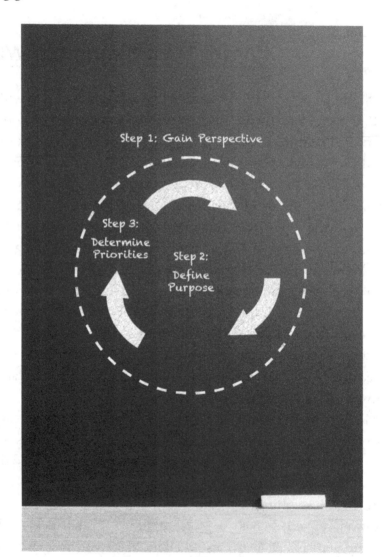

"I have to agree with Michael. We've gone through the prioritizing drill a hundred times, and it seems like all we do is create a longer and longer list of things we must accomplish," Bill added.

"Let's try this," Oliver said, "instead of trying to explain to you what I mean by priorities, let's just do it. Would each of you please take a clean sheet of paper from the stack I put out this morning?"

He waited while Bill, Michael, and Susan each secured a fresh piece of paper from the pile on the table. When everyone had a sheet, Oliver continued. "Take five minutes on your own to brainstorm a list of all the possible goals you and your team could accomplish. You can include things that are already on your plate, items you've been thinking about in the back of your mind, and perhaps some things that you've yet to consider, but might make sense to visit." He paused for a moment to let each of them digest what he said, and then he added, "Any questions? No takers? Okay, start."

Susan, Bill, and Michael immediately began creating their lists. Susan seemed to have no problem creating a laundry list of possible goals. She began work at the word "start" and continued writing down items until Oliver told the group that the five minutes had expired. Bill and Michael started off more slowly; however, Michael picked up steam as time went on and created a fairly lengthy list. Bill's list was the shortest with less than ten items.

After time had expired, Oliver said, "Okay, now that each of you has created your list, please take a moment and put a checkmark next to the items you believe will have the greatest impact on your customers' top priorities. Please limit yourself to no more than six checkmarks."

As he watched them work, Oliver reminded himself that this is where things start to get interesting. For most people, all the items on their list represent good things that they can do with their team, and no one wants to say no to a good thing. Susan, who was unwittingly prepared to prove his point, interrupted these thoughts.

"Why do we have to narrow the list to six?" she asked. "My paper is covered with goals that I think are important for us to accomplish."

"Let me see if I understand you," Oliver replied. "As you look down your list, you see a whole bunch of items that would be good for your team to accomplish?"

"Absolutely!" she enthusiastically responded.

Oliver nodded his head in acknowledgement of her excitement. "The reality is that this is where the problem begins for many teams. No one wants to say no to a good idea. In all likelihood, accomplishing good ideas is what has made each of you so successful in your careers." All three seemed to agree with this statement. "Getting good things done is what gets you promoted and increases your responsibilities. However, I'm trying to get you to separate the merely *good* ideas from the *truly great* ones. So as you look down your list, try to pick the six best possible ideas that you and your team can accomplish in the next twelve months or less."

His response seemed to satisfy Susan, and she returned to the task of placing a checkmark next to the top six items. As he watched her, Oliver chuckled to himself thinking, *Wait until I ask her to cut that list to four or five items.*

When they finished placing checkmarks next to the items, Oliver asked each person to take a moment to share the list they had created, placing special emphasis on the six items that received checkmarks. Each person went through their list and shared their ideas. Everyone seemed to agree with the others' decisions. The only exception came when Michael explained that he had placed a checkmark next to the goal called "improve communication."

Oliver stopped him, saying, "Michael, I totally agree that improving communication is very important, but I think you are going to find it hard to keep that as a goal for several reasons."

He paused and waited for Michael's response. Michael didn't say anything verbally, but his expression of disbelief showed that he questioned Oliver's comment.

By way of reassurance, Oliver said, "The problem with goals like communication, collaboration, trust, and so on is that they are hard to measure and often hard to impact in a way that doesn't distract from driving the organization forward. I can imagine that you can think of several things you can do to improve communication. However, I also believe that you would find in the end that many of those things create a lot of busywork for your team. Don't get me wrong, I'm all about improving communication, collaboration, and trust. I'm just *not* all about making them one of your top goals.

"What I've found," Oliver continued, "is that when you create a compelling goal for your team to work on and they work together to accomplish it, the by-product of that effort is improved communication, collaboration, and trust."

Oliver leaned in closer to Michael and said, "You played basketball in college. Think about the difference between a winning basketball team and a losing basketball team. My bet is that teams that win also experience higher trust, collaboration, and communication both on and off the court." With that comment, Michael put a line through the communication goal—enough said.

Oliver went back to his trusty chalkboard. He turned the knobs on either side of the board and rotated the entire surface to reveal the opposite side, on which he had pre-drawn instructions for the next step.

Prioritization Matrix

POTENTIAL GOAL	Feasible	Measurable	Meaningful	Easy to Under-stand	Effective	Financially Doable	TOTAL SCORE
	Can we get it done?	Can we tell if we won?	Is it important?	Does it make sense?	Will it help our team fulfill its purpose?	Do we have or can we get needed funding?	

SCORING SYSTEM

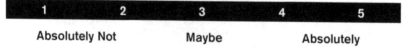

1	2	3	4	5
Absolutely Not		Maybe		Absolutely

Pointing at the chart, Oliver explained, "You can use a chart like this one to help you finalize the six remaining ideas, to find which ones are truly the best."

"Hold on," Susan exclaimed. "You mean we need to shorten the list more?"

"Yep, that's exactly what I'm saying," Oliver responded with a warm smile. "My suggestion is that less is more here, and my research supports that. I'd recommend that you shorten the list to the three to five most important goals. Listen, I know that narrowing the list of goals is tough, but it's essential and it's what the most effective leaders and teams do."

"Alright," Susan stated. She continued hesitantly, "I'll give it a try. How do we use the chart?"

"The first thing you do is list your six potential goals on the left side. Then going from left to right, score each of the potential goals based on how strongly you believe the possible goal is feasible, measurable, meaningful, easy to understand, effective, and financially doable on a scale of one to five, with five being high and one being low. Then tally the score for each potential and compare the scores. The form is pretty simple to follow. Let's take five minutes or so for each of you to complete it."

All three copied what was on the board and worked quickly to complete the *Prioritization Matrix*. They then shared the results with each other. As they shared their selected goals with their colleagues, they become more confident in the selection and in their ability to explain the rationale. Oliver told them to hold on to that confidence as it would be helpful when they discussed the goals with their teams and their boss.

Oliver's comment about sharing the goals with the teams raised a question in Bill's mind. "Oliver, when we work with our teams, should we simply walk in and say, 'Here are the goals, deal with them,' or should we ask for their input?"

"Yet another great question," Oliver said. "Both approaches have their pros and cons. Sharing the goal with the team and explaining that it is written in stone is certainly the fastest way to move through the process. It also allows you to provide clear direction about what you expect from them. The negative side to this approach is that you might lose buy-in from your team members if they feel this is *your* goal and not *theirs*. On the other hand, asking them to create the goals can often slow the process down and may take more than one meeting to solidify them. Of course, it's worth the investment of time if that is what it takes to get the right goal."

As his students finished their notes, he said, "Like everything else you approach in your role, it's about which approach is right for your situation. If you believe the goals are the right ones to tackle at this point, you may want to go in and say, 'Folks, I've been thinking about our priorities, and here are the five things I believe we need to accomplish.'"

"Ah, but won't that kill buy-in?" Michael asked.

"It could if you do it in a way that turns everyone off, but if you can defend your selection, you will be fine. Plus, when we get to the next step, you'll be asking them about how to accomplish the goals, and that's where the *real* buy-in takes place. Anyway, you know what I've found *really* kills buy-in?" Oliver asked.

"What?" Michael replied.

"When a leader acts like he wants input, but in reality he's just going to talk them to death until they finally select the goals he already has planned out in his mind," Oliver explained.

"I've seen that on more than one occasion," Susan added. "You're right, people can't stand that. They like it much better when someone comes out and tells them what needs to be done."

Oliver glanced at his watch and noticed that they were way over time. "I just realized that we're running late, but I have one last thing that I'd like to share with you before we call it a day." There were no apparent objections, so he after a slight hesitation. "A goal isn't a goal unless it is well stated. There are several different ways to do this, but you have to make sure you make it very clear what you want them to do and when you want it done. Let me give you an illustration. Let's say that I told you my goal was to improve my health. What would you say to that?"

"Well, I'd probably say that improving your health is good, but what do you want to improve?" Susan asked.

"You hit the nail on the head. I'd need to tell you what measure I was going to use to determine if my health improved. I could reduce my weight, improve my cholesterol, decrease my body mass index, or any number of other possible measures. The key is that I need to pick one. So, Susan, how would you feel if I said that I was going to decrease my weight? How would that settle with you?"

Susan appeared excited to respond. "I would say that was better, but how much weight do you want to lose?"

"And when do you want to lose it by?" Bill added.

"That's exactly right. A well-stated goal needs to tell you the gap and when you want to close it by. Plus, it needs to be realistic, and if you look at my waistline over the years, you will see that my commitment to accomplishing this goal is not very good."

Everyone laughed as Oliver patted his belly in jest.

They wrapped up the session by agreeing that each of them would meet with their teams to finalize their goals and to set up a meeting with their boss Sam to bring him up to speed on the work they had been doing with the process. Each felt confident that they would be ready to share with Sam by the following Wednesday, and if they could get time on his schedule, they were sure that he would be open to the conversation.

Chapter 14: Momentum

Early Friday afternoon over lunch at her desk, Susan reflected on Todd's involvement during last Friday's session and his quick, positive feedback on the team purpose statement. She felt that his participation indicated that he valued the discussion and wanted the team to have clarity of purpose. Her excitement about Todd's involvement was somewhat muted as she reminded herself that new habits take time to form and that glimpse of Todd's potential might turn out to be short-lived. As she finished her salad, she vowed to remain adherent to Oliver's process, in hopes that it would continue to positively impact Todd and the team.

A couple of hours later, Susan's team was assembled for their second session. She looked around the table at her teammates. "Let's get started," she began, a warm smile appearing. Being creatures of habit, all four of them sat in the same seats as the week prior.

"Thank you for your quick feedback on our purpose statement. I appreciated your input and believe we created a statement that explains who we are, what we do, and who we do it for. If his schedule allows, I'm hoping to meet with Sam Finch next week and share with him our purpose statement and the result of today's meeting."

"So what are we going to talk about today?" Kim asked.

"We are going to talk about our priorities. These are the top things we need to accomplish in the next year or less to fulfill our purpose and to have the biggest possible impact on our clients," Susan explained.

Deciding to maintain the momentum with Todd, she turned to him and thoughtfully inquired, "Todd, are you ready for another exercise?"

"Sure, why not?" Todd's positive response brought a smile to Susan, Kim, and Chris. As an HR professional in the government, Susan often wondered why people who start their careers with such passion and potential often grow cynical, almost resentful. She had seen it so many times and wondered if the process they were going through truly might help people like Todd return to an earlier enthusiasm about their jobs.

Pressing forward, Susan handed each of her team members a piece of blank paper. "Alright, I'm going to give each of you five minutes to complete our next activity." She paused for a moment, fully expecting Todd to object. No complaints emerged, so she continued. "I'd like each of you to write down a list of possible goals our team can tackle over the next twelve months. These can be things we're already working on, things we have discussed but have yet to accomplish, or simply anything you think might be a good goal for us to accomplish."

She asked if anyone was unclear on the task. All expressed that they understood what needed to be done. Susan glanced at her watch and waited for the second hand to tick into the twelve position. When it arrived, she announced, "Okay, begin."

Her team members jumped into the exercise with even more enthusiasm than the past week's activity. Time passed quickly as she watched their lists grow. After five minutes, Susan announced that it was time to stop. Following Oliver's lead, Susan asked each of them to place a checkmark next to the ideas they thought were most important, limiting each of them to no more than six checkmarks. Todd, Kim, and Chris each selected six items from their lists. She then asked them to rank the six items using the criteria Oliver had shared with her the previous day and then narrow the list to the three to five most important goals. Not being an expert at the process, a couple of her instructions required clarification, but all three of her team members eventually completed the activity.

When everyone finished, Susan explained, "What I'd like to do is have each of you share the goals that you ranked highest. When you're done, I'll come explain the items I selected when I did this activity yesterday. Chris, if you don't mind, will you please capture everyone's ideas on the board?"

"My handwriting isn't very good, but I'll give it a shot." He sprang to his feet and grabbed a marker to use on the dry-erase board.

Each team member explained their selected goals. Susan facilitated the discussion, asking the presenter to pause occasionally to ensure everyone understood what was being said and to ask questions to ensure clarity. Susan went last, explaining her list. When everyone had finished, they looked at the board to survey the results. Their seventeen "best" ideas were listed in Chris's somewhat legible handwriting.

Susan thanked Chris for his excellent work as the group's scribe. She stood and walked to the board as Chris returned to his seat. "Alright, we have seventeen things listed on the board. That's way too many," she explained. "We need to somehow narrow this list."

"I can narrow the list a bit," Todd said, pointing to the board as he continued. "If you look, each of us talked about the need to improve training delivery. Those can probably be combined into one goal, don't you think?"

All agreed, and the four items were cobbled into one concise goal statement. For the next half hour, they continued to reduce the list. In the end, the team had five well-written goals listed on the board.

With their newly defined goals, Kim made the comment that Oliver had said was coming. "Susan, I think we can all agree that these are good goals for us to achieve, but I'm wondering how we're going to get these done. As we've been talking, I've created a lengthy list of all the things we need to do in order to accomplish each of these goals."

Susan's response would have made Oliver proud. "Kim, you raise an excellent point, but today is all about the *what* we want to do, not the *how* we are going to do it. When we get together next time, we'll discuss the *hows* for each of these goals." Kim's expression conveyed her willingness to follow Susan's lead. Susan continued, "So, I have two things for all of us. First, if you have ideas about how to accomplish these goals, please hang on to them for our next meeting. Second, as we discuss the *hows*, we need to be willing to adjust the goals to account for workload, available funding, and a number of other constraints. I want to ensure that when we finalize these goals and our plan for making them happen that we are all confident that we will be successful. Does that make sense?"

"Not only does it make sense," Todd declared, "it makes perfect sense. I feel like we're often chasing our tails, responding to whatever new idea somebody else dreams up for us. But these things," he said, gesturing toward the board, "these are the ones that really matter. If we can really figure out a way to make these things happen, I'm fully on board."

The meeting ended a few minutes later, but Todd's comment stuck with Susan for the next several days. On several occasions she caught herself thinking, *Oliver really is on to something here!*

Chapter 15: Update Meeting

Sam Finch arrived in the conference room a few minutes before the meeting was scheduled to start. He wasn't exactly sure of the gathering's purpose, but after receiving the third of three invitations from members of his leadership team to attend a one-hour "Update Meeting," he knew a coordinated effort was underway. Typically, Sam would decline an invitation that didn't come along with an agenda. He learned this trick early in life, and he was confident that it had saved him hundreds of nonproductive hours over the course of his career. However, he was willing to make an exception to this practice because he valued Susan, Bill, and Michael. He was confident that they wouldn't ask for the meeting and violate his "no agenda policy" if they didn't have a good reason.

He entered the room and saw that his three direct reports had already arrived. Susan stood at the front of the room next to a screen with the words "Status Update" plastered across it. Bill and Michael, who were seated at the table, stood when Sam entered. He invited them to sit as he moved to his usual seat at the end of the table.

"Okay," Sam said. "I'm not exactly sure what this meeting is all about, but I learned a long time ago that when the three of you have something to say, it's always best to listen." His face brightened. "So what are we here to talk about?"

Without hesitation, Susan began. "Sam, first, thank you for taking the time to meet with us. We know that you have a busy schedule, but we think you'll find what we are about to share with you interesting." She paused for a moment, watched her colleagues nod in agreement, and then continued. "Do you remember a couple of weeks ago when several of us went out to lunch at the sandwich shop across town?"

"Yep, I remember that day well," Sam said. "The food was good, and the conversation was certainly interesting. Why do you ask?"

"Well," Susan said, a smile emerging on her face, "after we finished our meal, I slipped into a nearby bookstore to look for inspiration. Frankly, the discussion had left me a bit drained, and I was hoping to find something in there that would help me better understand our current situation and how we might better perform on Mr. Morgan's metrics. I believe you would agree we were all struggling that day as we grappled with how to meet his goals." She looked to Sam for a response.

"Yes, I'd agree. I guess you must have found a pretty interesting book, given the discussions we've had during our recent Monday morning staff meeting," Sam said, referring to the conversation that had started a couple of weeks earlier when Susan had asked Jane Hudson, Mr. Morgan's surrogate, to identify which of the metrics mattered most. That one question started the best dialogue to date on the subject, and it had seemed to change the relationship between Jane and the agency's leadership.

The moment Susan asked the question, Jane stopped her normal briefing and shared a draft of Mr. Morgan's strategic vision. The sharing continued during the most recent staff meeting when Jane presented a revised version of the metrics and provided further explanation. In the new presentation, the metrics were aligned to Mr. Morgan's "Pillars of Success," and Jane had added a weighting system for the metrics. This allowed the agency's leaders to see which goals had the greatest influence on the pillars. At once, Sam Finch and his leadership team began to better understand where they should put their efforts.

Sam's thoughts returned to the room as Susan answered his question. "Actually, it wasn't a book. It was a person. To put it more accurately, it was a person who has read a lot of books."

"A person?"

"Yes, a person. Actually, he's the store's owner. His name is Oliver Stanton. I asked him about the topic of performance improvement. Instead of selling me a book, he invited me to meet with him, saying that he had read numerous books on the subject of management and leadership, and at their essence, most of them say the same thing." A grin appeared on Sam's face indicating that he'd had the same thought himself. "Oliver explained to me that he has learned, both from reading and application, that there are five steps every leader should follow in working with a team."

Sam's face turned from agreement to skepticism as he listened to her presentation. "Susan," he interrupted, "it's great that Mr. Stanton has read a lot, and I'm interested in what you have to say, but does he have any practical experience?"

"The same question was running through my mind when I started to talking to him," she answered. "Actually, he has a great deal of experience. Years ago he started, grew, and then eventually sold a chain of bookstores called AC's."

"Oh yes, AC's, I remember that chain. I think it was a pretty big business at one point, before some other company came along and bought them."

"That's exactly right," Bill interjected. "But there's something else about this guy that makes him different. Beyond reading a lot of books and growing a business of his own, he also has an uncanny ability to take business-speak and make it work in our world. He takes the normal corporate talk and relates it to the challenges we face in government. "

Susan nodded in agreement with her colleague. "Now Oliver is back in the book business, but working with just the one small store.

He says that he's very content with keeping it that way and occasionally likes to share what he has learned with others."

"And you've been meeting with him?" Sam inquired.

"Yes, we've all been meeting with him." Susan motioned to her two colleagues. Both Michael and Bill nodded in agreement.

Michael added, "I was the last to join the group, and I have to admit, Sam, it has been very interesting and challenging."

Sam seemed to lose his skepticism as he listened to Michael. After a moment of reflection, he motioned for Susan to continue.

Susan used her presentation slides to prompt her efforts. With each click of the remote, a new slide appeared revealing another step. She briefly explained the three steps they had learned, the importance of each, and that Bill, Michael, and she had been working with their teams to complete each step.

Following the quick overview, Susan, Michael, and Bill shared their efforts to date with Sam. They then asked Sam for feedback on their work, explaining that they wanted to ensure that they were moving in the right direction before going on to steps four and five. They admitted that they weren't certain as to the last two steps but that they had a pretty good feeling what they might entail.

Sam was completely engaged in the conversation. He was amazed at the accuracy of their perspective assessment. Offering only a few minor suggestions, Sam believed their *Perspective Matrix* captured the most important points. "I have to admit," he said, narrowing his eyes as he concentrated on his thoughts, "I have been through many strategic planning sessions where experts have shared the results of lengthy external and internal studies, and I have yet to come across something as simple and straightforward as this."

When they presented their draft purpose statements, the trio explained that they had worked with their teams to craft and refine the statements. Susan highlighted that the discussion with her team was very positive and had helped all of them gain clarity. Michael added that his team members had already started posting the statement in their cubicles as a reminder of what the organization wants them to do.

"This last week," Bill began, "we started work on step three: determine priorities." He turned to face Sam. "I have to admit, this has been a challenging step for my team. Walking in the room, I assumed that we all knew the most important things to work on, but boy was I wrong. Everyone had a different opinion of what mattered most."

"Different in what way?" Sam asked warmly.

"The first thing I did," Bill explained, "was to ask them to grab a blank piece of paper and write down their ideas for the top goals the Budget and Finance team must accomplish in the next twelve months. The results were embarrassing." Bill paused to consider the fact that he had just told his boss that his team didn't agree on what was most important. His moment of concern quickly faded as he realized that Susan and Michael would likely reveal similar results. So he pressed on. "Keep in mind, there were four of them in the room, and I asked each of them to give me the top three to five goals. Worst case scenario: if they were all on different pages, they would come up with twenty different goals. That would be four people each stating five very different goals."

"Well," Sam asked excitedly, "what did you get?"

"I got twelve different answers. Honestly, they were all over the map. And you know what the most amazing thing was?"

"Go ahead," Sam prodded.

Sheepishly Bill continued. "As they went through the twelve different goals, all of them came from me. I was the source of all the ideas. I was the cause of the confusion on my own team."

Before Sam could say a word, Michael added, "Sam, I had the same experience on my team. There was a lot of confusion about the top goals. Don't get me wrong, the people could say the agency's mission statement from memory, but they were not in agreement about what we needed to accomplish in the short term to make everything else come together."

"Ditto," said Susan. "When I asked my people the question, I was confident that they would come up with the same answers, but they didn't. It became clear that the daily work, ongoing meetings, shifting priorities, and overall challenges of their jobs, and my job too, were causing confusion."

Susan clicked the remote, and the screen displayed, "Step 3: Determine Priorities."

As her colleagues turned to face her, Susan said, "With your permission, Sam, we'd like to share with you the top priorities each of our teams identified. Our hope is that you will provide us your feedback and direction to ensure we're on the right track."

They followed the same format used for the first two steps. Susan went first and explained her team's goals, followed by Michael and Bill. Susan presented four goals, while Michael and Bill each presented five. On occasion, Sam would stop the presenter to clarify an item or to challenge their thinking. The discussion was collaborative, and Sam found little that wasn't in alignment with his understanding of the agency. He was surprised that most of their goals required very little, if any, funding. Of the fourteen goals presented, only one had the potential to require funding beyond what was currently in the team's budget. At first he considered rejecting the goal because of the financial requirements, but he agreed to let the team to continue to work on it so they could identify exactly how much money they were talking about. Then he would make a final decision about approving or disapproving the effort as stated.

The entire conversation was of great interest to Sam. The final slide caught his full attention. Susan clicked the remote one last time, and the final graphic appeared. It provided a visual of how the three directorates' goals tied to Mr. Morgan's metrics. Two things became immediately clear. First, everything the teams had picked impacted at least one, if not multiple metrics. Second, the bulk of the selected goals connected *directly* to Mr. Morgan's top priorities as Jane had identified them.

Michael, Bill, and Susan had hoped that this final slide would "seal the deal." They wanted it to convince Sam to approve their teams' goals and to encourage them to continue the process with Oliver. Sam didn't disappoint. "So what do you need from me?"

"Glad you asked," Susan said with a smile. "We'd like your approval on these goals, of course with the changes you provided today. Also, we'd like to meet with you next week to share our progress."

Sam agreed to both requests, stating, "I had no idea what I was getting into when I walked into the room, but I'm glad I came. Please send me a final copy of the last slide once you insert the changes we discussed today. Also, shoot me an invitation for our next meeting. I look forward to it."

"Our pleasure," Susan replied.

Sam thanked them for their time and, as usual, departed the room on his way to another meeting.

Susan, Bill, and Michael spent a few minutes basking in the moment. "Well, I don't think that could have gone much better," Bill stated, delivering a rare high-five to his colleagues.

Chapter 16: Two Great Lessons

Oliver was deep in thought when his students arrived at the store. Even the jingle of the door's bell did not stir him. Susan's "Good afternoon, Oliver," startled him though. He looked up from his book to see Susan, Bill, and Michael standing at the counter. In typical form, Oliver ran his hand through his disheveled hair and peered at them over his reading glasses.

"Well, hello there," Oliver said, clearing his throat. "I didn't hear the three of you enter the shop." Turning to Susan, he added, "I told you when we first met that I could get lost in a book." He glanced at the regulator clock hanging behind him to check the time. It indicated that it was fifteen minutes from their normal start time. "The three of you are early."

"We have lots to share," Susan responded enthusiastically.

Bill added, "It's been an interesting two weeks."

"You've piqued my curiosity," said Oliver as he walked from behind the counter. All three noted he was dressed in his usual attire of starched khaki pants, blue button-down shirt, smock, and reading glasses. Per usual, everything was in place except the crop of hair perched like a nest on his head. "Let's get started."

The four walked to the store's back room along the way, Oliver stopped to say something too his colleague who would watch the store in his absence. While Susan, Bill, and Michael secured their usual seats, Oliver poured himself a cup of tea. Always the host, he offered tea, coffee, or water to his guests. All three declined. The host interpreted their rejection of a beverage less as an indication of thirst and more as a desire to get the discussion started. He was right.

As soon as he secured the last seat at the table, Michael began. "Each of us met with our teams over the last two weeks. Although bumpy at times, the discussions went well, and we were able to come to an agreement with our team members on our goals. After we solidified our goals, we then met with our boss to bring him up to speed on our efforts and gain his feedback."

Not one to let a question pass through his head without asking it, Oliver inquired, "I definitely want to hear about how the discussion went with your boss, but I'd first like to learn a bit more about your team meetings. May I ask a couple of questions?"

"Of course," Michael answered.

Oliver began questioning in his normal quizzical style. "When you say that the discussions were bumpy at times, what bumps did you run into?"

"I'd say we ran into two big issues. One of which came from the discussion I had with my people. The other surfaced as Bill worked with his team." Michael explained as he turned to Bill and asked, "Would you prefer to go first or second?"

"You've got the floor," Bill replied. "Just keep going."

"Fair enough. My team had no difficulty coming up with possible goals. In fact, they came up with a very long list of ideas. At first, I was surprised how many potential goals they listed. As they went through the list, though, I started to see that all of the ideas were well thought out and each of them could certainly make a difference. We went around and around trying to narrow the list. It was painful."

"I see," Oliver said. "It sounds like you were having a difficult time separating the good ideas from the great ones."

"Yes, that's exactly it," said Michael.

"So what did you do?"

"Well," Michael responded, "I did what you taught us. I remembered that it's hard to say no to good ideas and that people who are high achievers typically take on lots of things. I explained this to the group, and they agreed. Nonetheless, we hit a stalemate. Sensing that we weren't going to make any more progress, I suggested we stop at seven goals, take a break, and reconvene after the weekend. I encouraged each person to truly consider what mattered most and come back with the two items they would take off the list if they had to remove something."

"That sounds like a good approach," Oliver added. "How did that turn out?"

"We met on Monday, and everyone came with the two items they would remove. Guess what?" Before anyone could respond, Michael answered his own question. "With the exception of one person, everyone listed the same two items. The guy who didn't agree on both items did match on one, but not both goals. A brief discussion ensued. In the end he agreed, and we shortened our list to the top five things."

"Michael, I have to tell you, that is excellent work," said their instructor. "And you accomplished two things that some leaders struggle their whole lives to achieve. First, you demonstrated to your team that they needed to make the hard decision in order to place their best energy on the most important things. Second, you allowed them to work together and *with* you to make that informed choice. That's great work." Oliver turned to Bill and asked, "What was the challenge you ran into with your team?"

"I have to admit," Bill replied, "it was almost like my people were reading from a script, Oliver. They did exactly what you said they would do."

"And what was that?" Oliver asked.

"They kept getting into the weeds. Every one of them wanted to talk about how we would do this or how we would do that. Finally, in an effort to get them on track, I offered an analogy. Please forgive me if this was off target, but it seemed to work," Bill added sheepishly.

"No need to apologize," Oliver said. "We're in this together."

"Well, I told them that we were talking about finish lines, not how we were going to get there. I said, imagine if we were runners on a track team. If we were asked to run a medley race, our first questions would probably be, 'How far?' and 'How fast?' I told them that was the purpose of the planning step."

"Yes, I like that. Go on," Oliver urged.

"I then said that a future discussion would be about arm swing, stride length, and baton handoffs. It took a few minutes to sink in, but they got it. From that point on, anytime someone started getting too far into the details, someone would say, 'That sounds like a baton handoff,' and like magic, the conversation would work its way to the right spot."

Oliver stood and began walking toward the chalkboard. He reached for a piece of chalk. After selecting one from the trough at the base of the board, he turned to the others, saying, "That's exactly what we are going to talk about. How you and your teams will accomplish these goals. The baton handoffs, if you will." He flashed a smile at Bill.

Susan interrupted. "Oliver, hold on one second. We definitely want to learn about that, but we have yet to tell you the best part of the last two weeks."

She stopped him in his tracks. Oliver put the chalk down and retreated to his seat. "I'm sorry; I thought the three of you were finished. Please continue."

Over the next several minutes, Oliver learned about the meeting with Sam. They told their teacher about the decision to invite him to the meeting and of how Sam reluctantly attended. They shared their approach to presenting the information, Sam's engagement in the discussion, and ultimately his approval, with slight modifications, to their goals. Susan ended with, "And the best thing is that he wants us to continue to meet with him to discuss our progress." She looked Oliver directly in the eyes and with a slight smile added, "So...no pressure here, but we have to deliver."

HIGHLIGHTS

Step 3: Determine Priorities

"Priorities focus on identifying the key goals your team must accomplish to positively affect what matters most to those you serve and to simultaneously impact your team's purpose."

KEY POINTS:

No one wants to say 'no' to a good idea, but prioritization demands tough decisions.

Improved communication, collaboration, and trust are often the result of selecting and accomplishing an important goal.

When determining priorities, focus on what you want to accomplish, not on how you intend to do it.

LEADER CHECKLIST:

✔ Brainstorm a list of possible goals your team can accomplish

✔ Narrow the list to the top six goals

✔ Complete a Prioritization Matrix and select top goals by answering:
- Can we get it done?
- Can we tell if we won?
- Is it important?
- Does it make sense?
- Will it help our team fulfill its purpose?
- Do we have, or can we get, needed funding?

Step 4: Formulate Plan

Chapter 17: Listen to Your People

Oliver added the words "STEP 4: FORMULATE PLAN" to his evolving model on the chalkboard. In addition to the words, he added an arrow showing a connection between steps three and four.

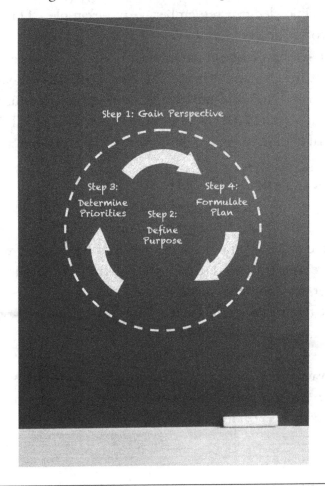

"The fourth step is to develop a plan to accomplish each goal." As he spoke, he returned to the board and wrote, "Project or Process."

"To do so, you must determine if you are dealing with a project or process goal. Project goals have a specific start and stop timeframe and involve a very specific deliverable. On the other hand, process goals deal with improving an existing process to reduce completion times, improve outcomes, and so on."

He waited a few minutes for Susan, Bill, and Michael to complete their notes and then continued. "I'm sure the three of you remember the example I gave the other day about setting a goal to lose weight." All three acknowledged, remembering the example. "Do you think that is a process or a project goal?"

After several silent moments, Susan decided to take a stab at the answer. "At first I thought it was a project goal, because you have a specific start and stop date and I could argue that your reduced weight was the deliverable. However, after thinking about it a bit, I think it's a process goal because there are things that you can do over and over to hit your target weight."

"That's exactly right," Oliver said enthusiastically. "To win on a process goal, you typically need someone to do something to some standard at some frequency. For example, to lose weight, I might need to run three miles at nine minutes each four times every week. Or I would have to eat no more than two thousand five hundred healthy calories per day. Does that make sense?"

"Yes, that makes perfect sense. How about a project-type goal?" Michael asked.

"Why don't you tell me?" Oliver responded.

"Always quick with the Socratic turn," Michael answered. He paused for a moment and responded, "Okay, I've got one. Let's say instead of setting a goal to lose weight, you set a goal to set up an exercise room in your home. In that situation, you would be dealing with a project where you wouldn't do the same things over and over."

"Yes, that's right—please continue," Oliver encouraged.

"If I were setting up a home gym, there'd be a list of things I would need to do, like design the layout, construct walls, pick out and install flooring, and purchase and set up the workout equipment."

"Right," Oliver interjected. "In the case of a project goal, you would need someone to do something by a certain date."

He returned to the board. Under the words "Project or Process," he drew two tables to capture the information they had just discussed. He then asked if Bill would be willing to help them complete the tables for each example goal. Bill rose from his seat and navigated his way to the board. Oliver handed him a piece of chalk, and with Michael's and Susan's input, he completed the matrices.

Process Goal Matrix

OVERALL GOAL: Lose 15 pounds by 12/31

Who?	Does What?	To What Standard?	How Often?
Oliver	Runs 3 miles	9-minute pace	3 times per week
Oliver	Eats	No more than 2,500 healthy calories	Each day

Project Goal Matrix

OVERALL GOAL: Set-up an exercise room in home by November 15

Who?	Does What?	By When?
Michael	Designs room and installs walls	September 30
Michael	Selects flooring and get them installed	October 15
Michael	Researches and purchases exercise equipment	October 21

"So here's the next step. Meet with your people and have them help you create a plan to make the priorities happen. As you do it, use your experience as a leader to determine if the plan is viable given the resources you have available and whether or not the timeframes are realistic. I would suggest that you then take the plans to your boss to gain his input and support."

"That's exactly what we're going to do," Susan said. "Do you have any final words of advice?"

"I sure do," Oliver replied. "Work to create a plan that is *doable*, not too complicated, and captures the repetitive behaviors that will have the biggest impact on the goal, or in the case of project goals, identify the most important milestones that must be achieved. And one last thing—listen to your people. They often have the best ideas about how to accomplish goals; the problem is they're rarely asked."

Chapter 18: Developing Plans

Susan's Friday was a busy one. Typically, the end of the work week was a bit less hectic than the beginning. However, from the time she returned to the office on Thursday until the start of her team's session Friday, she found herself running from one meeting to the next, with barely enough time to squeeze in the requisite paperwork, e-mails, and phone calls.

She was disappointed when it dawned on her late Friday morning that she was going to have to postpone her team meeting by at least an hour to get her head above water and attend the last minutes meetings added to her schedule. The last thing she wanted to do was send a message to her team that the process didn't matter, or that she would simply push it aside because of other demands. En route to a late morning meeting, Susan swung by her team's workspace to let them know of the delay. She found Kim, Chris, and Todd all at their desks.

"Folks, I hate to do this," Susan said with a slight grimace on her face, "but I need to postpone our meeting an hour or so this afternoon."

In typical form, Chris and Kim both said that the delay would be fine. Not surprising, Todd objected. "Do you really need to change the time?" he asked.

Susan felt herself stiffen as he asked the question. Over the past few weeks, Todd had become more positive about work and was starting to turn into the team player she'd envisioned. Trying to not be defensive, she said, "Yes, Todd, I'm sorry but we will need to start an hour or so late. Will that be a problem?"

She braced for his response.

"Actually, yes, it's a problem," Todd answered. "We've made some great progress the last few weeks. I for one find it very helpful to get our priorities straight, and I've been working on some ways for us to accomplish our goals. I'd just hoped that we could roll our sleeves up this afternoon and get going on our plans."

Susan was speechless. She just stood there.

Todd filled the dead air. "Is it okay with you if the three of us meet at our scheduled time to get things started? You can join us as soon as your schedule allows."

Susan responded, "Um...sure, that would be fine. Let me take a few minutes to share with you what we were going to do today so that way you can get going on your own. I'll join you as quickly as I can."

Susan pulled out several sheets of paper that she had put together after her last session with Oliver. One side of each page showed a table labeled "Process Goal." The reverse side had one labeled "Project Goal." The tables had columns labeled as per Oliver's instructions. Susan quickly explained how to complete each table. After answering a few quick questions, she headed off to her meeting, promising to join them as soon as possible.

★ ★ ★

When her meeting finished, Susan hustled out of the conference room as fast as possible and hurried to meet her teammates. When she arrived, she found all three wrapped up in discussion. In less than an hour, they had managed to draft plans for each of the four HR goals and were discussing how to present them to Susan. Her entrance bought the conversation to a close.

Obviously out of breath from her sprint across the office, Susan announced her arrival. "Sorry for not being here earlier. I made the mad dash here as soon as the other meeting ended. How's it going?"

"Great," Kim replied.

"Absolutely," agreed Chris, with the enthusiasm Susan had grown to expect.

"It's going very well," Todd added. "In fact, if you'll allow us, we'd like to share with you our plans for making our goals happen."

"Sure, that would be great!" Susan exclaimed.

One by one, they addressed the goals. Using a sheet of large white flipchart paper with hand-drawn versions of the tables on them, Susan's three direct reports presented how the team would work to accomplish the three project goals and one process goal. She was amazed at their work! For each goal, they had set a clear plan for accomplishing it. The timelines were realistic, the distribution of tasks appropriate, and the budget requirements minimal. She asked an occasional clarifying question and provided feedback as appropriate, but overall the plans were solid.

Oliver was right, Susan said to herself, *it is important to listen to your people.*

When they finished, Susan thanked them for their time and effort, adding, "Bill Engleman, Michael Thomas, and I are scheduled to meet with Sam Finch next Wednesday to provide him an update on our progress. Would one of you like to join me and present our plans?"

Todd chimed in immediately. "If it's okay with you, and if Kim and Chris don't mind, I'd like to volunteer."

With a smile, Susan replied, "That would be great!" Chris and Kim agreed.

★ ★ ★

That night Susan talked about the day's events over dinner with her husband. Greg listened with great interest. He then shared with her how well things were going with his team as he too applied Oliver's teachings. Both sat in amazement at the simplicity and power of the steps.

Chapter 19: An Unexpected Guest

Prior to the Monday morning staff meeting, Susan, Michael, and Bill conducted their weekly discussion to check progress and to help each other through any struggles or challenges.

All conveyed that they were surprised with how quickly the plans had come together. "It was interesting," Bill noted. "My team struggled with identifying the goals, but once we nailed those down, they were able to create plans fairly quickly. Oliver's right, teams do understand the details of how to get the work done...we just have to ask."

Michael agreed. "You're right, Bill, the plans did come together fairly well. One thing that stood out to me was that the goals that seemed too tough to some people last week seemed doable to them this week once we started putting a plan together. To help them break out of their thinking on the subject, I built on Oliver's example. I explained to them that I was told to lose thirty pounds by my doctor."

"That's highly unlikely," Bill interjected. "I don't think you've put on a pound since your college playing days."

"That's very kind of you," Michael said with a grin. "Now where was I? Oh yes, thirty pounds. So if the doctor told you to lose thirty pounds, you might feel overwhelmed, but if I said for you to run three times a week and watch what you eat, you would probably say that you could do that."

"I really like that example," Susan said. "How did they react?"
"They liked it too," Michael said excitedly.

"I had an interesting experience too," Susan continued. "One of my team members volunteered to attend the review session with Sam this week. Actually, he did more than volunteer. He nearly insisted that he join."

"Who was that?" Bill asked.

"Todd," she replied.

"Really? I always thought he had a bit of an attitude. I'm surprised he signed up for another meeting and face time with the boss," Michael said.

"Well, I won't talk specifics about his performance, but suffice it to say, he has been very enthusiastic lately."

Always the HR professional, Michael thought. *Susan would be the last person to talk about someone else's work performance without that person present.* He had always admired her for that.

The conversation came to a close as the start of the weekly staff meeting approached. Susan was the first to stand up from the table. She looked at her colleagues as they gathered their paperwork. "It's interesting," she said.

"What interesting?" Bill asked.

"Not that long ago, I dreaded going to our staff meetings. Today, I see progress and a path we can take together. I'm actually looking forward to this morning's discussion."

★ ★ ★

On Wednesday afternoon, Susan, Todd, Bill, and Michael waited for Sam's arrival in the conference room. The words "Status Update – Part Two" appeared on the screen behind Susan. Sam arrived right on time. They were surprised to see that he wasn't alone. Most surprising to them was to see who he had brought with him.

"Please sit down," Sam said as he entered the room. "I hope you don't mind, but I decided to ask a guest to join us today." No one could miss Jane Hudson in her bright red pantsuit.

Sure, the last few Monday morning meetings have been going well, but did Sam have to invite Jane to attend our status meeting? Susan thought to herself.

"I know what you're thinking," Jane said. "I'm not here to present any slides or share anything on behalf of Mr. Morgan. I'm simply here for my own education."

"Your own education?" Michael managed to ask.

"Yes, my own education," Jane replied. "During Mr. Morgan's weekly meeting, I shared with him the improvements I've noticed with your agency. I then asked Sam what he thought was the source of the difference in attitude and focus of some of his leaders. He told me about the meeting he'd had with this group." She gestured to those in attendance. "I said that it would be great if I could tag along to your next session so I could learn more about the process your teams are going through. So, I'm here to learn."

"Well, I don't know if we have much to teach you, but you're certainly welcome," Susan said, and with that, she started the presentation.

For the better part of the next hour, Susan, Michael, and Bill shared their teams' efforts to date. They emphasized the work their team members had put into developing realistic and timely plans to make their goals come to fruition. At one point, Susan's team member Todd joined the conversation, explaining how he found the process to be very helpful to him, and as colleagues they worked with Susan to better understand their customers, clarify their purpose, and establish goals that matter with a clear path to making them happen. He added that he had already seen some positive changes on their team.

As the session drew to a close, Jane thanked everyone for allowing her to participate and said, "It's interesting…as part of my job, I read a lot of books and attend seminars on performance improvement, but what you presented here seems to cut to the essence of what all those writers and presenters are trying to explain. I for one am very impressed with your progress and can't wait to see your plans put into action."

HIGHLIGHTS

Step 4: Formulate Plan

Leaders should listen to their people when formulating plans. Employees often have the best ideas about how to accomplish goals; the problem is they're rarely asked.

KEY POINTS:

Create plans that are doable, not too complicated, and capture the critical activities for success.

Ensure activities are assigned to specific individuals or roles. Assigning an activity to everyone is assigning the activity to no one.

Be realistic about timelines. People often have work responsibilities in addition to the goals. Don't lose sight of this.

LEADER CHECKLIST:

✔ Determine if the goal is a project or a process goal

✔ For project goals, complete a Project Goal Matrix to determine your plan by answering:
- Who?
- Does what?
- By when?

✔ For process goals, complete a Process Goal Matrix to determine your plan by answering:
- Who?
- Does what?
- To what standard?
- How often?

Step 5: Drive Performance

Chapter 20: It's More Than Flipcharts on Walls

As usual, Oliver started the session right on time. "Welcome back, folks. Today marks our last session together. I'm going to share step five with you, but before we start to talk about the last step, let me give you a warning. This is the hardest step and is really what separates the excellent teams from the mediocre ones."

Oliver returned to the trusty chalkboard and added the words "STEP 5: DRIVE PERFORMANCE" to his evolving image.

He paused and waited for his three students to write down the words. "The fifth step is where the rubber meets the road, or as I like to say, it's where teams realize that it's more than flipcharts on walls. What do you think I mean by that?" He waited a minute for a response. The blank stares around the table suggested that one wasn't coming, so he continued. "I bet over the course of your careers that each of you has spent time in rooms, probably not ones like this." He motioned to the cluttered back room in which they sat. "You're probably more accustomed to conference rooms in nice office buildings. I also bet that in those meeting rooms, you sat with colleagues and came up with big plans that you wrote on flipchart paper and placed on the walls. The words on the sheets represented hours of discussion and debate. Does this sound familiar?"

"Absolutely," Bill replied, "that sounds a lot like our annual planning session."

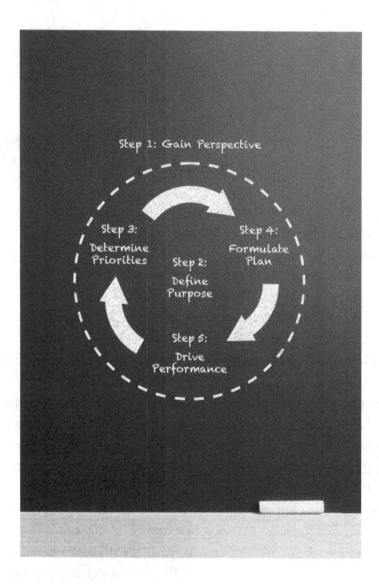

"Exactly," Michael confirmed.

"I *also* bet," Oliver continued, "that you can think of a time where six months after the planning meeting ended you found yourself wondering what happened to all the great ideas you discussed. Don't get me wrong, I'm not saying you weren't busy over the last several months. You were. However, you and your team simply lost sight of some of those goals because of the daily demands of your jobs. Does this sound familiar?"

"Sadly, it does," Susan replied.

"Okay, so we've all experienced something like this?" Oliver asked.

All three agreed with Oliver's question.

"I have one last bet to make," Oliver said. "I bet at a later time, you found yourself in another conference room, filling out more sheets of paper, and that those papers contained many of the same items that you had previously discussed. But this time you vowed that things would be different. Am I off the mark?"

"Not at all," Bill answered. "I can't tell you how many times I've seen this type of scenario. We get excited about a goal and the plan to make it happen, but we quickly find ourselves losing sight of both."

"I had this type of conversation during our team meeting this past week!" Michael exclaimed. "We were talking about our goals, and one of my more seasoned team members challenged me, saying that we've talked about these ideas for years and never got them done. He wanted to know what would be different this time."

"And what did you tell him?" Susan asked.

"I told him to give me a week to think about it. Then I prayed that Oliver would provide some insight that would help me answer his question."

Susan and Bill both let out a nervous laugh, suggesting that they shared Michael's sentiment.

Oliver said, "I'm going to use an illustration to explain what needs to happen to accomplish your top goals in the face of the day-to-day work. And I'm going to pick on you, Michael, to do so. Will that be okay?"

"Sure."

"Good. Now, pretend for a moment that you're ten years old again. You and three of your friends are shooting baskets in your driveway. You are just having fun, throwing up shots, acting silly, perhaps talking about a new song you heard or something you saw on television. Can you picture this?"

"Absolutely, that's how I spent most of my days as a kid."

"Okay, now after a while, one of your friends says something like, 'This is getting boring. Let's play a game.' He then points to one of the two other boys and says to you, 'Me and him against the two of you.' The first team to ten points gets a free ice cream from the losers.' Now, what happened to you at that very moment?" Oliver asked.

"A little switch in my head just flipped." Michael made a flipping a switch motion with his thumb and forefinger. "It went from *we're just playing around* to *game on, this really matters*."

"That's exactly right. Immediately the intensity goes up, your desire to score increases, you improve your shot selection, you start talking to your teammate, you come up with a game plan, and the list goes on. You simply become much more focused." Pointing to Michael, Oliver added, "Susan and Bill, look at Michael. Do you see a change in him right now as we talk about this?"

They both turned to look at their colleague. Oliver was right. Michael was now leaning forward in his seat, and he had become much more engaged in the conversation.

"That's the type of engagement teams need to achieve their best. Every person on the team needs to realize that the goal matters. Their individual contributions matter. We're keeping score, and they all have a role to play."

Oliver turned back to the board and drew two vertical lines making three columns. He labeled the columns "Individual," "Team," and "Leader." Under the word "Individual," he wrote, "Understand role and complete tasks." Below "Team," he wrote, "Discuss and track progress." In the "Leader" column, he listed "Facilitate process and assist team members."

"Just like the players on any sports team, the members of your team must understand their roles and complete critical tasks every week. This might sound easy, but it's not common practice."

The three students nodded in agreement.

"For example, my wife and I have two grown sons," Oliver explained. "I remember that when they were school age, they would sometimes wait until the last minute to complete a project. Even if the teacher assigned the work six weeks earlier, they would often be up the final night, trying to get the project done. They would be frustrated and so would my wife and I."

"That sounds familiar," Bill said.

"All *too* familiar, I'm sure," Oliver continued. "It wasn't because they were bad kids; it was just because their daily activities of school, friends, sports, and family kept their attention off the long-term goal of the course project. The only way to break this cycle was to get the boys to break the work up into segments and to complete the necessary daily and weekly tasks to get the project completed on time. My job as the parent was to make sure the process was moving along and that they had what they needed to succeed. This wasn't something I would do at the beginning of the assignment and then wait for the grade to show up on the project—it was something I would do every week."

"What do you mean, 'something you would *do* every week'?" Susan asked.

"I mean that every week, as the leader, I would have a huddle with my sons. We would discuss where things stood, how they were progressing, and what I could do to help. We'd talk about the good, the bad, and the ugly. What was and wasn't working well for them.

"To use another sports analogy," Oliver continued, "making this work for your teams is a lot like the game of football. What happens after each play?"

"The team huddles," Michael answered.

"That's exactly right. In a huddle, they quickly discuss how the last play went. A player might say, 'Great catch,' or 'You missed that block.' Then they look at the scoreboard to see where things stand and decide what play to run next. They confirm each person's assignment, saying things like, 'Run this route,' or 'Make sure you block that guy.'"

"And this is similar to what we should do?" Susan asked.

"Yes, it's very similar. If you want to accomplish your goals without losing focus on everything else that needs to happen at work, you move with the speed and intensity of a football huddle. Once per week, you need to check in with your folks and see how things are going to ensure that the process and project goals are staying on track and that you are getting the results you expect."

"So we need to add *another* meeting?" Bill groaned.

"Not another meeting, a football-type huddle. Make it quick, make it engaging, make it focused, and then make it over. A meeting like this is the only way to keep the goal moving and to not cause yourselves to sit back in another conference room a year from now talking about the same old goals you failed to accomplish this year."

"Okay, I get it," Bill said. "I'm the last guy who wants another meeting, but I agree." He glanced at his notes to ensure he understood the key points. "If we really want to accomplish these goals and move the metrics in the right direction, we have to make time for these hud-dles. I also agree that my job is to facilitate the process and to help my people win. Their jobs are to understand their roles and to perform them in the face of all the other stuff we need to get done. It won't be easy, but it does make sense to me."

"To help keep your teams focused," Oliver explained, "I suggest creating and using a goal tracking matrix. The simplest way to accom-plish this is to build on the process and project goal matrices you com-pleted during step four, planning."

Oliver rotated the chalkboard to reveal the back side of the sur-face. The information Bill had printed about losing weight and setting up a home gym during their last meeting remained. However, Oliver had some additional information to help with goal tracking.

"The first goal we talked about was a process goal," Oliver explained. "It focused on my losing fifteen pounds by December 31. I've added a couple of things to what Bill wrote down during our last meeting. First, I placed 'Where I should be' and 'Where I am' under the explanation of the goal. This allows people to see where we cur-rently stand compared to where we should be. This tells us if we are on or off track.

"Second, I added columns to the table for me to write down whether I met the daily or weekly requirements or not. I added four columns, because that's all I had room for on the board. You would need to put a column down for every week through the end of the goal. For this simple example, I put down a plus sign when I met the requirement and a minus sign when I didn't. It's quick and easy to read."

Process Goal Tracking Matrix
Overall Goal: Lose 15 pounds by December 31
Where I should be: Down 2.5 lbs (as of September 1)
Where I am: Lost 3 pounds

Who?	Does What?	To What Standard?	How Often?	Week			
				1	2	3	4
Oliver	Runs 3 miles	9-minute pace	3 times per week	+	-	+	+
Oliver	Eats	No more than 2,500 healthy calories	Each day	-	+	+	+

"Could we use something like a smiley face or a checkmark instead of the plus and minus symbols?" Susan asked.

"Absolutely!" Oliver responded. "I'm just showing the basic information. You can add whatever you want as long as it helps your team track progress. Now, let's take a look at the project goal."

Oliver pointed at the second table on the chalkboard and said, "The second goal dealt with setting up a home gym in Michael's house. Again, I kept this simple, and as Susan pointed out, you can add other things to help your team stay focused. For this one, I included an 'as of' date under the goal and 'Status' and 'Notes' columns to the table. You can see that I added information about what has been completed, whether or not it was done on time, and activities that are currently under way."

Project Goal Tracking Matrix
Overall Goal: Set up an exercise room in home by November 15
Results as of: October 1

Who?	Does What?	By When?	Status	Notes
Michael	Designs room and installs walls	Sept 30	Done on time	Room designed and walls installed 1 week ahead of schedule
Michael	Selects flooring and get them installed	Oct 15	Working	Picked up samples and discussing with wife
Michael	Researches and purchases exercise equipment	Oct 21	Working	Talked to rep at fitness store and have websites to visit

Bill, Michael, and Susan copied Oliver's additions to their notes from the previous session.

"Along with conducting huddles and using a tracking tool," Oliver continued, "I suggest you pick a date in the future, say in three to six months, for your team to present their progress to your boss. Having this date on the calendar is similar to having to turn in the homework assignment. It provides another level of accountability and lets the team know that we are *not* going to forget about the goal."

"That makes sense to me. Is there anything else?" Susan asked.

"Yes, the three of you and your teams have put much time and energy into the last several weeks, and you've made great progress. As I look at each of you, I get the feeling that you are both encouraged and discouraged by this final step. I understand—there is no quick fix. You're going to have to do the hard work of carving out time to talk, holding yourselves and your teams accountable every week, and making decisions that move teams from mediocrity to excellence. This will mean saying *no* to ideas you might have said *yes* to in the past. This will mean being a bit uncomfortable when someone misses a commitment and you have to address the situation. It also means you will have the ability to celebrate successes like you have never celebrated before and to build a team that can accomplish anything they choose to tackle."

He returned one last time to the chalkboard and rotated it so his five steps model reappeared for the group. He then added one last item, an arrow. This arrow connected step five to step three.

Oliver added, "As your teams accomplish their plans, each of you, as a leader, must ensure that the desired results are achieved, changes in the environment are considered, and new priorities are established to ensure ongoing success."

Oliver paused and looked each of his students directly in the eyes. "It has been an absolute pleasure getting to know each of you. I have looked forward each week to our meetings together. It's been thrilling each week to hear all that each of you accomplished. Please promise me that one or all of you will stop by at some point in the future and give me an update on how things are going."

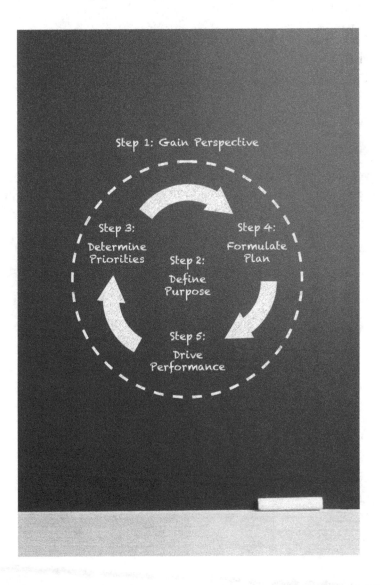

"Wait a second, Oliver," Susan interrupted. "When we first met, you asked me about our goals, then we met each week and discussed our progress, learned new information, and you helped us think through our challenges. Now you're asking us to come back in a few months and provide you an update on our progress. It sounds like you're using the five steps to teach us the five steps. Is that right?"

With a wink Oliver replied, "That sounds about right!"

Chapter 21: Getting Results

The door swung open, and the old bell rang once again. Susan recognized the familiar sound. Although she hadn't entered the store in over four months, the memorable noise transported her back to the first time she entered the store. The shop hadn't changed a bit. She glanced at the piles of books scattered throughout the store. Susan smiled to herself as she realized that the place she once viewed as a disorganized mess was now one of warmth and learning.

She saw Oliver sitting on the stool behind the counter. More accurately, she saw Oliver's full head of hair behind the counter. As always, he had his head down and his mind lost in the book that lay before him.

Susan waited a few minutes before she let her presence be known, simply watching the man who had become her friend and teacher doing what he enjoyed most. When it became evident that he was not going to notice her entrance, Susan made her way from the door to the counter. Her arrival occurred at the same moment as a particularly humorous part of Oliver's text. He lifted his head in laughter at the author's jest and caught a glimpse of Susan.

"Well, look who's here," Oliver said. "It's been way too long. How are you doing?"

Oliver sprang to his feet and worked his way out from behind the counter. His outfit didn't disappoint. The pressed khaki pants, blue button-down shirt, smock, and glasses were exactly what Susan expected. They gave each other a brief hug as Susan said, "I've been doing great. I'm just sorry I haven't stopped by sooner." She offered a warm smile.

"That's okay. I know you have a lot going on. What brings you by today?" he asked.

"Yes, I've been very busy, but before things get busier, I wanted to share with you what has happened since my last visit and our discussion about driving performance. Do you have a few minutes to talk?"

Not surprisingly, Oliver answered, "My time is your time."

Susan explained that a great deal had happened since the last time they met. She, Michael, and Bill met with their teams and discussed what it would take to perform at the highest level. The discussion with her team went well, and she received everyone's commitment to the process. From the very first huddle and progress review, she saw a difference in the team's performance.

"As we've implemented the five steps, I've seen my team more engaged in this process than ever before. Sure, we have some challenges, and it's a bit uncomfortable when we get behind schedule on a project goal or fail to perform as agreed upon for a process goal, but we talk about, learn from it, and recommit to staying on track."

"That's wonderful," Oliver responded.

"It is wonderful. In fact, one of my team members, who had the worst attitude and was on his way to losing his job, has really turned a corner over the last six months. He has gone from someone I was happy to avoid to someone I seek out when the toughest tasks come our way."

"Do you mind if I ask a question?" Oliver asked in his usual polite manner.

"I'd be surprised if you didn't," Susan replied.

Oliver smiled and said, "What do you think has caused him to change?"

"I asked him that exact question," Susan replied. "He told me that he changed when he saw that we were going to get clear on what mattered most to the team and that he and his colleagues had a voice in setting both the goals and the approach to accomplish them. He said that until that point, he was simply moving paperwork across his desk each day and it really didn't matter if he showed up for work or not. Now he tells me that he feels a sense of purpose in our work and knows how our team will drive the organization's results."

"Susan, that is wonderful. I'm so happy for you and your team. I bet you're also more fulfilled."

"Absolutely! I now look forward to the Monday morning meeting and seeing how we, as an agency, are advancing on our goals."

"So is the whole agency on board with the five steps?" Oliver inquired.

"Not everyone," Susan answered, "but soon they'll all be using the steps!"

"Tell me more," Oliver prodded.

"About four weeks after we finished our last session with you, my boss, Sam, said he began to see a real separation between the teams that Michael, Bill, and I lead from other teams in the agency. While everyone else was still operating under the old model of doing things, we were more focused and our teams were beginning to accomplish things no one thought possible. Old ideas that were discussed for years were starting to come to fruition. It was very exciting."

"I bet it was."

"So Sam asked the three of us to share the process with our colleagues. We didn't do as good a job as you did, but we did manage to share the basics and get everyone started. It wasn't perfect, but the entire agency started making positive strides, and the metrics began moving in the right direction."

She continued, "I just came from a half-day meeting with Sam, his boss who created the metrics, and all of my colleagues."

"How did that go?"

"All in all, I think it went very well. We've made some tremendous progress over the last several months, and those above me in the organization expressed their pleasure with our efforts. Don't get me wrong," she added, "we still have plenty of work to accomplish, but we're seeing movement and things feel different."

"That's wonderful, Susan. I'm so happy for you, Michael, Bill, and all of your people."

"Well, there *is* one more thing," she said.

"What's that?"

"My boss has asked me to put together a training program for the entire agency to teach everyone the five steps and to provide them the tools they need to follow the process time and time again. I still have work to do, but I came up with the title for the process. I'm going to call it Team Planning & Execution."

"Wow! That's amazing," Oliver said, a huge smile appearing on his face. "Would you be willing to share the materials with me when you finish? I'd love to see them."

"Absolutely," Susan replied. "You will get the first copy off the printing press."

"I'm looking forward to it." He paused for a moment to gather his thoughts and continued. "Susan, I'm often delighted by the wonderful people who find their way into this old bookstore, but you, my friend, are a cut above my other customers. I've so enjoyed our time together and hope that you have learned as much from the experience as I have."

"I've learned so much more than you could imagine," Susan said.

The conversation continued for a few minutes until Susan excused herself to get back to the office. She promised not to go so long between visits. They hugged goodbye, and she walked toward the entrance.

As she reached for the doorknob, Susan looked over her should to see Oliver buried back in his book. Susan shook her head in amusement. At that moment, the door opened and she nearly ran headfirst into a man in his thirties. They exchanged pleasantries as they passed one another. Just before the door closed behind her, she heard the man ask, "Excuse me sir, do you happen to have any books on employee engagement?"

"Certainly, we have a number of books that address employee engagement," the familiar response came. "But first, when you say employee engagement, what do you mean?"

Step 5: Drive Performance

"Performance is the hardest step and is really what separates the excellent teams from the mediocre ones."

KEY POINTS:

It is critical to keep the goal in front of your team to ensure they don't lose sight of it.

Team members need to understand that the goal is there to stay and not simply a random or passing thought.

Everyone must understand the role of the individual, the team, and the leader when it comes to accomplishing goals.

Develop and utilize a Goal Tracking Tool to measure progress.

Don't be afraid to have the tough accountability discussions.

Teams must conduct huddles to stay on track. It is critical that they be consistent, focused, and fast.

LEADER CHECKLIST:

✔ Ensure every team member is clear on the priorities and the plan to make them happen

✔ Develop and use a tracking tool to measure progress

✔ Meet frequently to discuss progress and ensure everyone remains focused on the goal

✔ Set a date to review the results of the effort and celebrate successe

Author's Notes

For the last decade, I have had the pleasure of working at Wedgewood Group. Without question, my colleagues are true professionals in every sense of the word. They, along with our clients, inspire me every day. Although my name is listed on the cover of this book, the text would not exist if it wasn't for the continual support of my wife and business partner, Jamie, our two children, Alex and Clay, and all of my Wedgewood Group colleagues. Jamie and I met in college, and she has been my best friend and the love of my life since our first conversation.

True, the characters depicted in this book are a work of fiction; however, the various concepts and processes outlined are very real. They represent a compilation of our efforts working with federal and not-for-profit organizations to help them maximize the passion and potential of their people and drive meaningful results. I appreciate each of my colleagues for the role they played in helping this book come to fruition. I would especially like to thank Kevin Curran for partnering with me on a number of client Planning & Execution sessions over the years and helping me to work through and refine our Team Planning & Execution Process. Lastly, I extend my warmest thanks to Colleen Kielty and John Barone for shaping this manuscript. Their feedback was candid, insightful, and much appreciated.

About Wedgewood Group

Wedgewood Group is a change management and strategy consulting firm. Since 2001, our experience in the field of strategic planning and workforce development with government and not-for-profit organizations, our team of highly capable professionals, our deliverables, and our methods have set us apart from our competitors. As we work with government and not-for-profit organizations, we exhibit several behaviors that are core to who we are:

- **We develop the right solutions for clients who aren't driven by profit.** Just because profits aren't a push does not mean performance isn't expected. Wedgewood Group helps our clients demonstrate their successes through the creation of measurable objectives that tie the day-to-day work of team members to the overarching strategies of the organization.
- **We start with the facts, not our assumptions.** Through research, analysis, and surveys, we first determine what the facts on the ground are. We then collaborate with our clients to determine where the organization should be, and the best way to get there.
- **We don't lecture, we listen.** We work with team members at all levels of the organization to make sure that all the initiatives undertaken are relevant, realistic, and can be appropriately resourced.

- **We create to effectively communicate.** Through the development of polished and effective collateral pieces, the strategies, goals, successes, and initiatives of an organization can be effectively communicated to the team. The transparency and internal marketing efforts bring the team together in driving the execution of objectives, goals, and strategies.
- **We are proven, professional, and passionate people.** Our team consists of proven performers who have worked at high levels of the government, in fast-paced environments, and in positions of consequence. The mix of backgrounds and experiences gives Wedgewood Group an unmatched team that has delivered time and time again for our clients.

To learn about Wedgewood Group, please visit us online at www. wedgewoodgroup.com.